CONTENTS

MORE THAN A GAME

THE GLORIOUS PRESENT AND UNCERTAIN FUTURE OF THE NFL

BRIAN BILLICK

with MICHAEL MacCAMBRIDGE

SCRIBNER

New York London Toronto Sydney

SCRIBNER
A Division of Simon & Schuster, Inc.
1230 Avenue of the Americas
New York, NY 10020

First Scribner hardcover edition September 2009

SCRIBNER and design are registered trademarks of The Gale Group, Inc.,
used under license by Simon & Schuster, Inc., the publisher of this work.

For information about special discounts for bulk purchases,
please contact Simon & Schuster Special Sales at 1-866-506-1949
or business@simonandschuster.com

The Simon & Schuster Speakers Bureau can bring authors to your live event.
For more information or to book an event contact the Simon & Schuster Speakers Bureau
at 1-866-248-3049 or visit our website at www.simonspeakers.com.

Manufactured in the United States of America

1   3   5   7   9   10   8   6   4   2

Library of Congress Control Number: 2009027874

ISBN 978-1-4391-3048-3

*For the hundreds of dedicated, talented people
who played a crucial role in the success of the football teams
I've coached, yet never got the chance to stand on a podium
and hold the Super Bowl trophy*

MORE THAN A GAME

THE KNIFE'S EDGE

The night was cold and raw, with winds gusting up to forty miles per hour, but as I walked through the chill to the sideline of the M&T Bank Stadium on December 3, 2007, I was reminded of how much I love the game of professional football.

The team I coached, the Baltimore Ravens, was free-falling through a painful losing streak, standing at 4–7 after five straight losses. People were calling for my job and questioning whether I'd lost my team. We were going into a game against the 11–0 New England Patriots, the most imposing team the league had seen in more than twenty seasons, and few people outside the Ravens' locker room gave us much of a chance.

But all week long, we had felt otherwise. In watching game films, we'd seen teams like the Redskins and Bills shy away from challenging New England's defense, failing to exploit the deteriorating speed of their aging linebacking corps. We knew that with our bruising offensive line, we could hammer the Patriots and wear them down. I emphasized all week that a ten-play touchdown drive would be better than a ninety-yard bomb.

With the hopes for building on our 13–3 success of 2006 already dashed, there was a sense throughout the team that this game might be the season's last great stand. No one said it out loud, because they were professionals and we still had a month of games left to play, but the feeling was palpable. It was Monday night and we were at home in front of a national television audience. The raucous Ravens fans were their usual boisterous selves. The team was keyed up as well, and particularly focused on this night. Just a week earlier, three of our players—University of Miami alums Ray Lewis, Ed Reed, and Willis McGahee—had buried their close friend Sean Taylor of the Redskins, who'd been slain by an intruder at his home in Miami. They'd dedicated this game to Taylor's memory.

So we were at an emotional peak, and from very early on (after the Patriots' Ben Watson dropped a touchdown pass in the end zone, forcing New England to settle for a field goal), I had the sense that we would be in the game for the whole sixty minutes. And what a game it was. It had a reckless, frantic quality, with bodies flying around and making frightening hits, exactly the way former players like to *remember* they played the game. There were big plays, big mistakes, players performing in a barely controlled frenzy (and sometimes—as when our frustrated linebacker Bart Scott threw a referee's flag into the stands, incurring a fifteen-yard penalty—just beyond it).

Tempers were running high on the field and on the sidelines. After our quarterback Kyle Boller threw an interception, the Patriots' Rodney Harrison, one of my favorite players in the game, ran by me on the sidelines and launched into a profanity-laced rant about my quarterback and my team. I responded with a sarcastic kissy-face right back at him, just to let Rodney know that I loved him and that he could kiss my ass.

In the locker room at halftime, the mood was electric, because our players knew we could stay with the Patriots. The game was tied then, and remained so after three quarters. We scored a touchdown early in the fourth quarter and then dug in, hoping we'd done enough to prevail. The Patriots kicked a field goal midway through the fourth quarter and before you knew it, we were asking our defense to hold them off one more time.

No one on our coaching staff was surprised. We had known all along that even if we could wear them down, control the tempo, and take a lead into the end of the game, the Patriots' quarterback Tom Brady would bring them back. We were just hoping we had enough left defensively to make the key play at the end. As it turned out, we did. On fourth and one during the final drive, we stoned Brady on a quarterback sneak.

Only it didn't count. Our defensive coordinator, Rex Ryan, had called time-out from the sidelines a split second before the play occurred. He had always had the latitude to do so, and he'd saved us from disaster with these timely bailouts in the past. This time, though, the time-out nullified the play and gave the Patriots another chance. But the defense came up again, stopping Heath Evans for a one-yard loss, as the stadium rocked with the roars of the Baltimore faithful.

Only *that* didn't count either. False start on New England, so the play was nullified. Now it was fourth and six, though it felt like sixth and six. *How many times would we have to stop them?* Brady called a pass, our defensive alignment was perfect, we had receivers covered all over the field. But Tom Brady is Tom Brady. He scrambled for twelve yards and the first down, and in the process crushed our spirit. Moments later, he threw a touchdown that won the game for New England.

The mood in the locker room afterward was anguished. We knew we'd given it our best, and I struggled for the words to adequately recognize the immensity of the effort. Some players said frankly that the season was over—and thereafter a few played as though that was the case. Some accused the NFL and referees of bias in favor of the Patriots. It was the inevitable talk of a group of proud players who were facing the reality of a year's worth of work going down the drain.

Meanwhile, as I left the stadium, I knew the loss would only increase the calls, within the media, for my firing. But I wasn't really worried about this; I'd signed a new four-year contract earlier in the year, and our owner, Steve Bisciotti, had assured me, both publicly and privately, that he was determined to keep the leadership in place.

As it turned out, that didn't count either. After two more losses, we won our last game of the season, against the archrival Steelers, and I showed up at the Ravens' training facility in Owings Mills, Maryland, the next morning, ready to start gearing up for the off-season. It was then that a somber Ozzie Newsome, my close friend and the Ravens' general manager, gave me the news: I was being fired. Bisciotti, when he spoke to me, couldn't have been nicer.

There's a theory in the NFL that after nine or ten years of hammering home the same philosophy, a coach is going to be tuned out by his players. That belief might have led to the firing, but in the final analysis, it was our 5–11 record that sealed my fate. I have been asked the question: What if we'd won that game, been the only team in the league to beat the Patriots in the regular season? Would I still be coaching the Ravens today? My guess is that probably I would. But I could be wrong. That's the knife's edge that this game is played on, for players, coaches, general managers, and owners.

Now here's the other side of that knife: Back in December 2007, I wasn't the only one taking heat. Just a week before our game with the Patriots, you could have heard rumblings about another team that seemed to have lost its way. The mediocre club had a dead man walking for a head coach, and its performance, in an ugly 41–17 home loss in late November, was so inept that it caused longtime observers not merely to wonder why the embattled coach was still in place, but also to ask pointed questions about whether the young quarterback (who threw four interceptions that day) would *ever* develop, what the new general manager had been thinking during the off-season, and why the franchise was having so much difficulty finding a sense of direction.

Barely two months later, that same imperfect, floundering team stood as the world champions of professional football. The improbable rise of the New York Giants, who'd barely managed to get into the playoffs as a fifth seed, is an example of the remarkable parity in the modern National Football League, a theme largely obscured during the 2007 season as the Patriots became the first team to march through a sixteen-game regular season without a loss. The Giants, viewed as something of a playoff impostor even in the league's weaker conference, the NFC, began to cohere in December and, once the playoffs arrived, consistently outperformed their favored opponents, first beating Tampa Bay, then knocking off their nemesis, the Dallas Cowboys, then going to Green Bay to vanquish the Packers in an Ice Bowl sequel that turned out to be Brett Favre's last stand as a Packer. Finally, they traveled to Super Bowl XLII and did what the Ravens couldn't quite do, ending the season-long unbeaten run of the Patriots. It was the second time in three years that a wild-card team had run the table, winning three road games and a Super Bowl to capture the Lombardi Trophy.

Want a more recent example? Take a look at what was being said about the Arizona Cardinals after their horrendous 47–7 loss to the New England Patriots on December 21, 2008. That desultory performance was their fourth loss in five games, and they hadn't been competitive in three of those games. Though they'd lapped the field in the worst division in pro football, the NFC West, the Cardinals were almost universally dismissed as impostors who didn't *belong* in the postseason. Then head coach Ken Whisenhunt refocused his team, and they charged through the NFC playoffs, beating Atlanta at home, Carolina on the road, and Philadelphia back at home, to earn the franchise's first ever Super Bowl trip. Against the Pittsburgh Steelers in Super Bowl XLIII, they showed remarkable resolve and fought to the very end before losing a classic.

The Giants in 2007 and the Cardinals in 2008 underscored the razor-thin edge between the very best teams in football and the merely good, as well as the hyperintense level of competition throughout the league. Fifty years after he'd first spoken the words, pro football was still living up to the proclamation of storied commissioner Bert Bell, who said, "On any given Sunday, any of our teams can beat any of our other teams."

In pro football, those given Sundays have grown richer, more popular, more pressurized, more documented, more dissected, and more competitive than at any time in the league's history. Indeed, the game is riding high on more than fifteen years of labor peace, shrewd stewardship, and savvy marketing. At the age of eighty-nine, the National Football League is experiencing another golden age.

Yet I fear that the league itself is like those 18–0 Patriots heading into Super Bowl XLII: vaunted, unvanquished, but strangely vulnerable. And in this case, the stakes are far greater than merely an undefeated season.

The National Football League is a closed universe, in many ways, but it's also a highly complex, densely interconnected one. It's the universe that I've aspired to, matured in, and thrived in. It's the universe, eventually, I was fired from. It's a universe I may well return to someday, because it's one of the most fascinating, challenging, competitive, rewarding fields I know.

But it's hard to see it clearly from the center. For nine seasons, I saw football from the inside, as the head coach of the Ravens. I was privy to a tremendous amount of information that never leaves the locker room or the boardroom, but also insulated from much of the criticism and conflict from above and from outside the organization.

Losing my job was a shock, and a blow to my ego. But I'm a football coach, and it's our nature to try to turn every problem into a challenge, every setback into an opportunity.

So within days of the firing, I decided I wanted to stay busy and remain involved in the game. I accepted an offer to serve as a game analyst for the Fox Network, and agreed to do some pieces on strategy and tactics for the NFL Network.

I decided to write this book as well, because I wanted to explain the game better to those who don't fully understand it and, frankly, I wanted to better understand the game myself.

One can hear the mixture of curiosity and bewilderment—on blogs, on sports radio, in living rooms, and in the newspapers—a nagging sense that beneath all the athleticism, spectacle, and obsession, there's something *else* going on down on the field, forces of which fans and the media are only dimly aware. That part I know. When I walked out on the field to coach a game, I was aware of that entire mix: the strategy, the financial pressure, the injuries, the players' attitudes, the owner's preoccupations, the media's assumptions, the dense array of hidden details that can subtly turn a game in one direction or another.

But I thought that by taking a few steps back and examining the game from some other angles, I could understand the whole living organism more fully. I wanted to ask a billionaire what possessed him to buy a football team. I wanted to better see the world of football through the eyes of general managers, scouts, players, fans, and the league office. I wanted to try to get a sense of how all the complicated pieces fit together, because sitting in my coach's chair, and dealing with the unforgiving schedules that we live our lives by, I hadn't had the time to examine many of the most pressing questions with the attention they deserved.

There are multiple issues confronting the NFL in the coming years. There's the lingering enigma of the nation's second-largest market, Los Angeles, which has been without an NFL franchise for more than a decade. There's the persistent problem of how the league can best police off-field player behavior while at the same time redoubling its efforts to provide players with life-management support. There is the perennial question of how to make safer a game that is played by faster, larger, stronger athletes than ever before. There is the challenge of policing the use of steroids and performance-enhancing drugs. There is the question of how best to care for physically debilitated retired players, the aging warriors whose stark accounts of inexplicably uninsured health problems became front-page news in recent years. There is, as well, a range of issues left unresolved about expanding the reach of the game, to other platforms, other media, and other markets around the world.

But the biggest unanswered question, dwarfing all the others, is the fate of the collective-bargaining agreement, which was extended in a contentious meeting in March 2006, and which the owners voted to open early in 2008, making 2009 potentially the last year of the NFL's current salary structure. Without another extension, 2010 becomes an "uncapped year," after which, in the absence of a deal, antitrust law almost dictates that the owners will have to lock out the players and shut down pro football in 2011, until an agreement is reached.

So this is an attempt to better understand pro football today, by breaking the modern game down to its elements, in hopes of shedding more light on the relationship between those parts. I have learned that while there is always room for improvement, the universe of pro football has attained a rough equilibrium. In short, the system has worked. And to the wisest heads in the game, what's most worrisome about a pending negotiation is that both sides are agitating for major changes.

"I just hope we can keep all the pieces together," says one longtime club executive. "Because if it falls apart, I'm not sure that we'll ever be able to put it back together again." The future of the sport lies in the hands of the men who run the game itself. What will occur over the next two years is nothing less than a war for the future of the game, a pitched battle for the soul of football.

"YOU OWE ME $40 MILLION!"

When Dick Vermeil was hired to coach the Philadelphia Eagles in 1976, he came with a reputation for unflinching commitment and a single-minded dedication to preparing football teams for games. Vermeil didn't compromise. He was notoriously oblivious to the outside world, and famously unbending, and had advanced in his profession because of these qualities.

His first boss in pro football was the mercurial Eagles' owner Leonard Tose, an irascible, somewhat unstable raconteur who'd made his money in the trucking business. Tose was famous for firing coaches and administrators on a whim. Vermeil realized early on he needed to manage the relationship, both for his own security and to protect his team from Tose's impetuous temper.

So on many Friday evenings, when Vermeil was set to go home to his wife, Carol, he instead accepted Tose's invitation to stop by the owner's office for a nightcap. The first time he did so, he found Tose well into his happy hour.

"Have some Scotch," Tose told Vermeil, as the coach sat down.

"Thanks, Leonard, but I don't drink Scotch," Vermeil said cheerfully. "But if you've got some wine, I'd love a glass."

Tose frowned. "I don't have any wine," he said.

This happened a couple of times, without variation. Something had to give.

Tose never did stock his cabinet with wine. Instead, Vermeil—the uncompromising oenophile from the wine country in California—learned to adapt. "I started drinking Scotch," he says.

That, in a nutshell, tells you what you need to know about the balance of power in professional football: Players play. Coaches coach. Owners own. Some owners are more visible, some less so, but they are still the ones who need to be satisfied. These are, after all, *their* football teams. And because of that, accommodations are made up and down the line. A good owner isn't going to win the Super Bowl for you—any owner is too far removed from the film room and the field of play for his influence to be that decisive. But a bad owner *can* lose you one, either by undercutting or overruling his front office or coaching staff, or by being so impatient that he sabotages his own team.

In any case, the notion that owners just write the checks couldn't be further from the truth. From general managers on down to the players, people in football learn that the owner is a presence who needs to be reckoned with.

When I started coaching the Baltimore Ravens in 1999, I figured out fairly quickly that my life was going to be easier if I could regularly explain myself to our owner, Art Modell. Art had been in pro football for nearly forty years, and he knew the game. But he was not impervious to the suggestions of people who *didn't* know the game or who did not know how to filter the information they were given.

Like most owners, Art was very passionate about his team

and had specific ideas about how it should be run. He was quite emotional after games, win or lose, and subject to hyperbole either way. If we won, I might be informed that I was the second coming of Vince Lombardi. If we lost, it seemed there was always some action that needed to be taken: I should fire a coordinator, start a different set of players, whatever tinkering we could do to get back on the winning side.

In either case, Art was not above making his comments public, and the local sportswriters knew it. I figured if I could take the brunt of whatever Art was upset about, it would save me a great deal of time I might otherwise have had to spend later fixing whatever problems might arise if an unchecked Art spoke off the cuff and his words blew up in the *Baltimore Sun*.

So I made it a point, after my postgame talk to the team, and press conference and shower, to stop up at Art's box. I went in there and took those hits so I could make Art understand how and why things happened the way they did. Art was going to have an opinion and I just wanted to make sure that opinion, to the degree it could be influenced, was influenced by me rather than his limo driver or his barber.

Even while grumbling, Art remained very respectful to me. One time I was visiting with him in his office and he was venting his displeasure with something going on during the season. When he realized he was pounding on me pretty good, he softened his remark by saying, "but I'm not talking about *you*."

"Well, Art," I said. "There's only the two of us in this room, so if you aren't talking about me I think you're being entirely too hard on yourself."

There's a wide range of ownership styles. The most hands-on owner is the Cowboys' Jerry Jones, who effectively operates as the team's general manager. Jones attends every game, like most owners, and almost every practice, unlike most. He stood up in front of the Cowboys on the first day of training camp in 2008 and said, "I can be anywhere in the world I want to be today, and I can be doing whatever I want to do. I choose to be here, with you."

On the other hand, owners also can be effective by hiring smart people and then getting out of the way. Arthur Blank, the owner of the Atlanta Falcons, was a wealthy football fan when he bought the team in 2002. Arthur went through quite a learning curve with his star player, Michael Vick, convicted of running a dogfighting ring, and a head coach, Bobby Petrino, who bailed on him and the team for a college job before the end of the 2007 season. But he made a couple of strong hires in 2008 with Tom Dimitroff as general manager and Mike Smith as head coach (for the record: Mike is my brother-in-law). They in turn made the right call in drafting quarterback Matt Ryan with the third pick in the 2008 draft.

When Blank hired Smith, he explained that he wanted to be kept abreast of what was going on with the team—through weekly, hour-long postmortems the day after Falcons' games—but beyond that, he was at Smith's service. "I told him, 'Look, I'll do whatever you want. You want me here, I'll be here. You don't want me here, I won't be here. Whatever works for you, because I'm here for you to be successful.' In my opinion, the owner needs to reflect what the head coach really requires, because the coach is the CEO of the football team, not the owner."

But that's only if the owner *wants* the coach to be the CEO, and that distinction makes all the difference. Owners shape their club's universe.

And even great owners can lose their way. For years, Al Davis was among the shrewdest men in football. Then, all of a sudden, he wasn't anymore. Take a look back at the Oakland Raiders' first-round draft choices this decade and you'll see a series of grievous mistakes that turned 2001's Super Bowl team into a mockery. One of the owner's jobs is to make sure whoever is making those draft-day decisions makes good ones. And if the owner himself is making those decisions, he'd better be right. Too often, Al has missed in recent years.

But that's only half of it. One way to tell that an owner is losing his grip is that in-house, behind-the-scenes matters don't stay behind the scenes. The 2008 season began with Raiders' head coach Lane Kiffin and Davis tangling in a war of not-for-attribution statements. Davis took action and fired Kiffin, but if you have to fire your head coach five games into the season—whether it's for losing or insubordination or both—something's gone terribly wrong. (The Raiders weren't the only team that went off rails in the middle of the season; the St. Louis Rams and San Francisco 49ers fired their coaches by the midway point, and the Detroit Lions fired general manager Matt Millen not long after.)

As the infighting got worse in Oakland the first few weeks of the 2008 season, with Kiffin and defensive coordinator Rob Ryan barely on speaking terms, and staff morale at an all-time low, I asked one Raiders' assistant if he'd ever thought of just taking his concerns and grievances straight to Al himself. "Oh, no," he said. "You don't pet the tiger."

After visiting Davis in Oakland a few weeks later, I was left with this: the vision of a brilliant giant of the game who no longer had the acute judgment he once possessed and who, unwittingly or not, had surrounded himself with people who could only agree with him, or who didn't feel comfortable contradicting him.

• • •

Now, here's where it gets difficult: For pro football to be successful, these men and women who are so powerful in their own element must learn to be partners and listen to thirty-one other people who are just as powerful. That dynamic shapes the agenda of the National Football League.

Commissioner Roger Goodell, like his predecessors Pete Rozelle and Paul Tagliabue, is a formidable, influential figure. But he doesn't drive the agenda the way Rozelle used to—no commissioner can do that these days. To a greater degree than ever before, the modern NFL *is* the group of thirty-two owners, and it's impossible to understand the way the league works without understanding that central fact.

For better or for worse, most of the people who owned pro football teams in the fifties and sixties were running a family business. The team was the primary source of income for Tim Mara and his sons with the New York Giants, for George Halas in Chicago and Art Rooney and his sons in Pittsburgh. Even if football wasn't the sole business, as with the Colts' Carroll Rosenbloom, the Rams' Daniel F. Reeves, and the Cardinals' Bill Bidwill, it became their *main* business, their passion. And the investments were minimal: The eight owners who started the American Football League in 1960 paid twenty-five thousand dollars each for their franchises.

The NFL owners were also bound together by a powerful institutional memory. Many of them had been in the league during World War II, when some teams and even the league itself had to consider suspending operations. They had needed a zealot's love for football because, during the lean years, that was the only way franchises survived. Bert Bell, when he owned the Eagles, used to hawk game tickets from the traffic median on Broad Street. Even owners who came into the game in the sixties had the shared suffering of the war between the NFL and

AFL, which nearly killed teams in both leagues even as it was increasing the popularity of the sport as a whole.

I came into the league hearing stories about and meeting these legendary patrician figures—second-generation scions like Wellington Mara and Dan Rooney, and American Football League founder and Chiefs' owner Lamar Hunt—each of whom had made major financial sacrifices for the greater good of the league. They set the tone that Pete Rozelle always tried to establish ("think league first") and they made it clear, on numerous occasions, that to them pro football was both more than a game and more than a business.

But in the past twenty years, the profile of the average NFL owner has changed drastically. As franchise values have escalated, so has the net worth of people buying into the league. The league features fewer sportsmen and more business tycoons, men who have made their riches in the modern economy. For owners like Steve Bisciotti in Baltimore and Steve Ross in Miami—men whose net worth is measured in billions—a new football franchise is an incidental, almost vanity, purchase.

The new breed of owners can be smart and engaging, but often they are cut from a different cloth. In spring 2008, I asked John Moag, the savvy sports lawyer who orchestrated the sale of the Miami Dolphins to developer Steve Ross, to arrange a meeting with the new owner. I wanted to ask him the simple question, "Why buy an NFL team?"

I finally got the chance to meet Ross in New York early in 2008 and was ushered into his office atop the Time-Warner Center, which he built. As he got off the phone I extended my hand to introduce myself, but before he shook my hand, he pointed his finger at my face and blurted, "You owe me $40 million!" As I looked at him quizzically he repeated, "You owe me $40 million!"

I reached into my pockets and replied, "I'm a little short on cash—would you take a check?" With that, Ross smiled and told me the story of his purchase of the Dolphins. He thought a deal was in place late in fall 2007, before the Dolphins beat the Ravens for their only win of the season. The victory made Dolphins' owner Wayne Huizenga sentimental, and though he'd already agreed on terms with Ross in principle, he told him after the game, "I can't leave these guys. The deal is off."

It took three weeks and $40 million more to close the sale.

Ross could laugh about that because he could afford to. Today's challenge for new owners is less about net worth than about liquidity. NFL rules require that even in an ownership group, a single person must have more than 50 percent of the stock—corporate ownership is still not allowed. Because of that, owners must be able to put up an extraordinary amount of cash to afford a modern NFL franchise.

There is a natural tension that exists when a group of old-guard owners (many of whom came into the league before it was a moneymaking machine) cross paths and sensibilities with new-guard owners (many of whom came into the league *because* it was a moneymaking machine, and paid dearly for the privilege).

Back in the early nineties, when Jerry Jones was setting his own agenda with stadium sponsorships, many owners thought he was the devil incarnate. But Jones's savvy marketing became the model that the rest of the league followed.

On the other hand, new isn't always better. When the Washington Redskins' owner Daniel Snyder bought his team in 1999 and began signing high-priced free agents, other owners were disturbed by his impatience, haughty manner, and strategies they felt were shortsighted. They were right.

As of yet, the Redskins' disappointing performance on the field hasn't prevented Snyder from enjoying what is among the most profitable franchises in the game. But there has yet to be a bar argument settled by someone saying, "Yeah, but the Redskins made more money last year!" In sports, the bottom line that fans care about is the one on the scoreboard.

"Right now, we have too many owners who just don't understand the issues in detail," says one longtime member of the old guard. "Some of them don't understand, period. Our founders knew, and the guys who pulled together, they traveled on trains, they knew. It's essential that owners understand the aspect of what we have here, which is a partnership, and what we create is a precious commodity that we all generate together."

As the game has grown more prosperous, the stakes have increased, right along with the pressure.

When the new stadium that will house the New York Giants and New York Jets opens in 2010, twenty-four of the thirty-two teams in the NFL will be in stadiums that are either brand-new or have been extensively refurbished (as in the case of Green Bay and Kansas City, which chose to renovate classic structures) within the past fifteen years. That's a tremendous amount of growth. And it has led, in turn, to a tremendous amount of debt. The era of easy money set these deals in motion.

"The debt levels today are much, much, much higher than they were fifteen years ago," says Ravens' president Dick Cass. "The limit is $150 million [per team], but you get waivers on that limit to build a stadium, and that debt is backed not just by an individual club but by the league on top of that. So there is a lot of debt in the league today."

Most NFL franchises are valued at nearly $1 billion today, and many teams carry more than a quarter or a third of that amount tied up in debt. In the case of three of the most valuable franchises in the sport—Dallas and the two New York teams—those figures are even higher. The Giants and Jets have a total of $1.5 billion in debt tied to their new stadium, and the Cowboys are highly leveraged from the building of their new stadium, which opened in summer 2009.

So if you love football, and are concerned about the future good of the game, you start to notice the accumulating signs of danger.

A group of new owners who lack the crucial institutional memory of their predecessors . . .

A growing level of debt that causes concern both within the league and among lenders . . .

The most visible franchises in the league being the ones that are most exposed . . .

A dismal economic climate in which everyone wants to reduce their debt load . . .

A corollary downward drift in ticket demand, ad revenues, and many other crucial financial indicators . . .

In short, a perfect storm of events within and outside the game, and a coming collective-bargaining negotiation that promises to be the most difficult and contentious in decades.

To understand how we got here, you have to consider what has changed about pro football since the present economic system was put in place in 1993. That visionary deal, which brought free agency to the players and a salary cap to the owners, ended a bitter, divisive decade dominated by strikes and lawsuits, and the end of labor discord provided the financial stability the league needed to thrive.

The first real glimpse into the modern economics of football came in 1994, with the sale of the New England Patriots, a losing franchise on the field that had been losing money at the box office as well, with an apparently gloomy financial future and an unfavorable stadium situation. Despite all that, the Patriots sold for a record price of $172 million, to Robert Kraft, a longtime Patriots' season-ticket holder and also, as it turned out, a savvy businessman.

This transaction was eye-opening to me. At the time, I was a young assistant with the Minnesota Vikings, and assumed I understood how pro football economics worked. The Patriots had seemed a cursed franchise. Billy Sullivan, the original owner, was the least wealthy of the members of "The Foolish Club," the American Football League owners who challenged the established NFL in 1960. Sullivan sold to Victor Kiam, the electric-razor magnate, who developed a reputation as a boorish caretaker of the franchise. Kiam, in turn, sold to James Orthwein, who, it quickly became clear, was intent on moving the franchise to St. Louis. The entire situation—team, stadium, tradition—was a mess.

Then Kraft stepped in, for the record sum. His reasons for buying the team were sentimental and civic, but also profit-minded. By the time the Patriots were sold, the NFL had emerged from the nightmare of litigation and work stoppages that had marred the 1980s. With labor peace, the salary cap that came with it, and richer TV contracts, teams could now more accurately project a good deal of their expenses and income.

Their basic revenues (the long-term TV deals, ticket revenue, other league revenue) were either fixed or highly predictable. Teams' expenses, limited by the salary cap, were also fairly predictable. As one highly placed NFL executive put it, "That defined margin between the revenue that you could almost certainly count on, and the cost that you could almost certainly count on, left a lot of money sloshing around in the system. As it happens, a lot of clubs didn't use that to book net income that they would then put into their pockets. They bought team planes, they built practice facilities, they put the money from football back into football."

After a damaging round of franchise movement in the mid-nineties, the league stabilized, grew smarter and more aggressive in terms of marketing opportunities, and capitalized on its attractiveness as a TV enterprise, pitting the networks against each other (just as Pete Rozelle first did in the sixties) to increase the value of each NFL TV contract. With the new guard of aggressive, debt-ridden owners leading the way, they also struck more aggressively at maximizing league income.

There is much to recommend the league's new way of doing business. In the early nineties, the NFL's licensing business was a nightmare of different companies, some of which (Pro Player and Starter) went out of business. By the end of the decade, different teams had deals with different companies, with Nike, Adidas, Puma, and Champion all outfitting some teams. Then the league consolidated all those outside deals into one exclusive leaguewide deal with Reebok, which would pay $250 million over ten years, far more than the total from the separate deals that had been in place. (A few years later, the NFL would do the same thing with computer gamemaker EA Sports, and its dynasty John Madden Football game, opting for more money through an exclusive deal than they would get with any number of nonexclusive deals on the open market.)

By early in the twenty-first century, all the leading indicators—TV revenue, ticket sales, stadium revenue, ancillary revenue—were good, and the league was flush.

That set the stage for the 2006 CBA extension negotiation,

which, tellingly, was extraordinarily difficult *despite* all the positive factors. Paul Tagliabue and National Football League Players Association executive director Gene Upshaw had been negotiating in earnest, forging a partnership, for more than a decade. Their paradigm of cooperation brought the league unsurpassed profitability.

But even with all that goodwill, the talks came down to the eleventh hour. Upshaw, exasperated by the owners' intransigence, finally made a last offer, a take-it-or-leave-it proposal, then boarded a plane to Hawaii. Tagliabue, spending every last bit of the political capital he'd accumulated over seventeen years, pressed hard to get the deal done.

And the deal got done.

"The perception is that we are fabulously profitable for many years," says one league executive. "So labor sees this, particularly in the form of increasing franchise values. They see it in owners' planes getting bigger, team facilities getting better. They pressed for more at the very time that our growth in revenues was starting to slow, and they got it."

But the extension changed the environment for the owners. In the previous deal, the players received 64.25 percent of defined gross revenues (DGR), based solely on broadcast revenues, ticket sales, and merchandise sales. The new agreement gave the players just 59.5 percent, but that was of *total* revenue, not just of DGR. With that, the owners' profit margins began to diminish.

That's one reason why the owners, in spring 2008, voted to reopen the negotiations two years early. And why all around the league in 2008, you heard people fretting over the possibility of an uncapped year in 2010 and a complete lockout in 2011.

The 2006 deal also had a powerful unintended effect on

smaller-market teams. The salary cap, for the first time, was calculated as a percentage of all team revenues, including most stadium revenues, the income item in which there is the greatest disparity among clubs, and which is largely unshared. When the salary cap had been determined by DGR, the money that big-market, new-stadium teams such as Washington and New England were making on stadium revenue had no direct bearing on the salary cap. But with all revenue going into figuring the cap now, smaller-market teams were put at an additional disadvantage. Revenue from new stadiums, which wasn't being shared equally among the thirty-two teams, *was* being used to calculate a growing leaguewide salary cap level that they still had to pay. Put differently, small-market teams had to spend a much greater percentage of their total revenue (at times more than 65 percent) than big-market teams to put a competitive team on the field.

At the time of the deal, the NFL also expanded its own supplementary revenue-sharing plan, with the fifteen highest-revenue clubs essentially subsidizing the fifteen lowest-revenue clubs to the tune of nearly $200 million a year. Inevitably, the direct payments from richer to poorer *felt* different from a revenue-sharing arrangement such as the TV contracts, which simply took a portion of money paid to the entire league and divided it equally among thirty-two teams.

Did the deal signed in 2006 end profitability? No. One league source estimated that thirty of thirty-two teams made money in 2007. A *Forbes* magazine report estimated that thirty-one of thirty-two teams were profitable. But the climate had changed, and the owners were wary.

"The owners, I will tell you, are very skittish," said one owner. "It's not Paul's fault, it wasn't Gene [Upshaw]'s fault, it wasn't the union's fault, but for a whole variety of reasons, the owners signed off on this agreement without a complete understanding of what it meant."

The owners soon found that practically speaking, the new deal greatly limited the freedom they'd previously had to use profits to invest further in the game. With 60 percent of all revenue now going to player salaries, their margins were cut, and this changed the way they viewed the deal.

"If you look at the agreement that we signed in 2006 it really by different accounts added three or four percentage points to the labor costs," says one league executive. "But three or four percentage points is a lot of money, and it was the money that had been sloshing around in the system. Four points out of $7 billion [the NFL's annual revenue] is $280 million. Bang, just like that, it goes out of the system. The money that was available for owners to build practice facilities and buy planes and pay coaches was just gone."

And by 2008, a new mind-set was starting to develop, as the owners were becoming much more cost-conscious about league expenses. For the first time in forty-five years, there were cutbacks at NFL Films, the league's film studio, which had both documented and glorified the game, and played an integral role in the sport's rising popularity. Rather than merely covering its expenses, the league now wanted NFL Films to be profitable. The league also shut down its developmental league, NFL Europe, though it cost franchises just $1 million per year and was an incubator for playing, coaching, and officiating talent.

And anyone paying attention could see more elements of the perfect storm coming together.

Growing disagreement between small-market and large-market franchises . . .

Gene Upshaw's untimely death in summer 2008, delaying by at least nine months the beginning of meaningful negotiations with the union . . .

Growing resentment from some new owners that the league didn't have their best interests in mind when the previous deal was struck . . .

And the ticking clock that says if a new deal isn't negotiated by March 2010, the league's salary cap will go away . . .

Meanwhile, the face of NFL ownership was changing. The fall of 2006 was a somber time for the fraternity of NFL owners. Barely a year after Giants' owner Wellington Mara had passed away, the Chiefs' owner and AFL founder Lamar Hunt died of prostate cancer. At Hunt's wake in December 2006, Paul Tagliabue approached Colts' owner Jim Irsay and said, "Well, this is your time. The guys that mentored you are pretty much gone."

Tagliabue was right. Now the league has a majority of owners who were not involved in professional football in the eighties, when the strikes of 1982 and 1987 tore the league asunder. They can't remember scenes like the one in which Chiefs' great Otis Taylor, then a scout for the team, crossed the picket line and exchanged words and then fists with Jack Del Rio, one of the team's active striking players, leading to the two men grappling on the ground, in a picture that was in almost every newspaper in the country the next day. They can't remember the hot summer day in Baltimore when Colts' All-Pro lineman Chris Hinton, wearing a hood over his head, ran to the bus carrying the Colts' replacement players and smashed out a window with a towel-covered hand.

Yet the backbiting, the recriminations, the anger remain in

the minds of the old-guard owners, and these memories often supersede pride, competitiveness, or false bravado. "It's inconceivable that we could put ourselves through something like that again," said one owner.

The Colts' president of football operations, Bill Polian, was in Kansas City, as a scout, for the 1982 strike, and in Buffalo, as a general manager, for the 1987 strike. "Labor disruption is an industry term," he says. "When you translate that to the fan, that means his favorite player is tarnished. His team is disrupted. But what we're in business to do is to entertain and please and involve the fans—that's what we do for a living. So if you constantly erode that bond between the fans and the players in the franchise, if it becomes labor problems and a disruption of the product on the field as opposed to rooting for the Buffalo Bills or the Oakland Raiders, or the New England Patriots, or whomever—you've broken a connection with the fans."

So there is a dichotomy among today's owners that goes far beyond more than half of them having no direct memory of work stoppages. It has to do with perspective. As the Dolphins' new co-owner Steve Ross sees it, the fact that many NFL teams are owned by second- or even third-generation families means he now has a new round of business partners who were born into riches rather than earning them. The old-guard second- and third-generation owners, on the other hand, can respond that because of the rising value of franchises, they're now in the company of a new batch of owners who may have succeeded in other businesses but know little or nothing about football.

And it's clear that whatever happens with the players, the owners must reconcile their own differences to a greater degree than they have. Gene Upshaw once observed, "From our position this is not a fight between the league and the players. This is a fight between ownership. The owners have to decide how they want to do business going forward amongst themselves. Once they do that, we can then figure out what the players have a right to."

For much of the past year, what I heard was younger owners sounding concerned, but confident.

"We're facing potentially an uncapped year in 2010," says one owner, who has been in the league for less than a decade. "You know, that's a scary proposition. On the other hand, the basic business is very healthy. It continues to grow 7, 8, 9 percent a year, somewhere in that range. I'm not talking about this year but under the normal set of circumstances for a long period of time. So it is a situation where the pie gets bigger and bigger. At the end of the day, between the owners, the players, the management, coaches, everybody, there is enough—the pie is big enough where it can be thoughtfully chopped up in a way where everybody gets a piece. Now if you're in an industry like the auto industry today, you're just shit out of luck. Many cars that are being made are being made overseas, so it's a different industry, condensing dramatically in the United States. We're not in that business. The NFL is healthy relative to any other sport."

Maybe that determined optimism will hold sway once the intense negotiations start. But over the past year, I also heard many older, more established owners sounding grave. As one longtime owner, talking about his new colleagues, put it, "They hear the concept of 'think league first.' But they're not so sure about it. That's the only thing we can continue to work toward. It's harder for some of these new people. They *say* they believe it. I don't know if they truly believe it."

"DON'T FALL IN LOVE WITH YOUR OWN PLAYERS"

In the world of pro football, there are few jobs better than the one Bill Polian has fashioned for himself.

The president of the Indianapolis Colts oversees all football and administrative aspects of the franchise and is among the most respected executives in the game. His record as a manager will land him in the Hall of Fame one day. He built the Buffalo Bills team that began a run of four Super Bowl visits in the late eighties, made an instant contender out of the Carolina Panthers in 1996, and in 1998 came to Indianapolis, where in the most competitive era in the history of pro football, he's created the most consistently excellent team in the sport. The NFL's winningest club over the past decade, the Colts have won at least twelve regular-season games for each of the last six years (no other team has ever done it more than four years in a row), and they have a Lombardi Trophy on their shelf.

The team's owner, Jim Irsay, has given Polian wide latitude to run the organization as he sees fit. In the team's recently renovated training facility on the outskirts of Indianapolis, Polian has been next door to Tony Dungy, widely hailed as the best coach in pro football, and in 2009, after Dungy retired, Jim Caldwell, Dungy's longtime understudy.

Down the hall, as the team's vice president of football operations, is Polian's bright son Chris, who will someday work as a GM in his own right.

On the field, thanks to an unsurpassed record of draft-day work, Polian surveys a young, deep organization, and the best quarterback in football, Peyton Manning.

In the off-season, Polian is among the most respected voices on the powerful competition committee, which oversees the rules of the game.

In short, you can't find a better football mind in a better situation than the one Bill Polian is in right now.

And yet, as I sit with him at the Colts' complex one November Saturday morning, and ask him if he's enjoying himself as much as he used to, he doesn't even hesitate before answering.

"Noooo way," says Polian, definitively. The game is still absorbing, but it's not nearly as much fun.

Polian is enjoying it less not because he's old and cranky—though he has earned a reputation as a prickly, combustible old hand, someone who commands respect at league meetings and fear in game-day press boxes. He's enjoying his job less because, day in and day out, he has a job that pulls him away from the sport he loves and toward the business he only barely tolerates.

His experience mirrors that of most of the men who have general manager duties in the modern game. In the past generation, no job in American sports has changed more than that of the general manager in pro football. It was a difficult job to begin with, and in the past fifteen years, the position has become more demanding, more frenetic, and more pressurized.

For much of the twentieth century, baseball was regarded as the sport in which general managers were most important. They oversaw the club's farm system, they negotiated contracts, they went to exotic locales in December for the wheeling and dealing of the winter meetings, then made the crucial decisions on managers, free agents, and trades.

In pro football, coaches made all the crucial decisions until the sixties, when Tex Schramm created the blueprint for the America's Team dynasty of the Cowboys, showing the benefit of taking the longer view. Because the Cowboys put so much emphasis on personnel evaluation, most teams that followed suit made their GMs glorified personnel chiefs. They'd travel much of the regular season, staying out of the head coach's way and scouting talent on America's campuses, then spend part of the off-season negotiating contracts, but mostly gearing up for the draft. Then it was three months of golf in the summer.

The job description was transformed in 1993, when labor and management reached the collective-bargaining agreement in which a salary cap and free agency were implemented.

The change was long overdue. Free agency had been part of baseball for nearly two decades by then, but the NFL's owners had stubbornly blocked it, settling for half measures, like the so-called "Plan B" free agency, instituted in 1989, which allowed NFL teams to protect the first thirty-seven players on their roster. At the time, when coaches were grousing about not being able to control each and every player on their team, the Giants' avuncular GM George Young commented to one aide, "You think you don't like Plan B? Wait till you see Plan A."

With real free agency and a salary cap, as stipulated in the 1993 collective-bargaining agreement, both the rules of how to build a team and the job of the builders changed dramatically. Suddenly, the balance of power between owners and players shifted. It wasn't enough to draft the right players. Teams now had to figure out how to *retain* those players.

The stockpiling of proven talent—think of the Steelers' trio of All-Pro linebackers in the seventies, or the 49ers' pair of future Hall of Fame quarterbacks in the late eighties and early nineties—proved impossible in the new era. In essence, evaluating your own players became a constant job, no longer a binary choice between Keep and Release but instead a nuanced, multilayered evaluation that took into account many variables: a player's value to the team, value on the open market, the cost to re-sign him, the consequences for the following year's salary cap of doing so, position scarcity if he wasn't re-signed, chance of promoting similar talent from within the organization, chance of signing comparable talent from outside the organization.

One thing became quickly clear: Teams would not, could not stay together in the manner that they had in the past. Trying to keep a veteran-heavy unit entirely intact almost guaranteed that you would run up into the cap sooner rather than later.

"Before free agency and the cap, the job came with small print that said, 'Don't fall in love with your own players,'" says one longtime general manager. "After that, it switched to capital letters, in neon."

With the celebrated free-agency campaign of the Eagles' All-Pro defensive tackle Reggie White in 1993, the paradigm of the new age was set: Big-money free agents toured the league, were wined and dined by coaches and executives, gave lip service to finding the "right fit," then invariably signed a fat, bonus-heavy contract with whatever team offered the most money. But for every successful free-agent signing like White, who helped push the Green Bay Packers to a Super Bowl, there were at least ten like the Bills' defensive mainstay Bruce Smith, whose skills had waned by the time he got to Washington, and who proved to be an overpaid burden on the cap-strapped Redskins.

"There were always going to be mistakes made in the learning curve," is how Ozzie Newsome puts it. "That was part of the theme of the first two or three years. We had never been in an era where you couldn't spend as much as you wanted. And so now, do you sign your younger players early? Do you go to shorter-term deals? Nobody had any track record."

"We were all gluttons at the start," says another GM. "We all—well, most of us, anyway—learned that you really had to understand how to project players into your situation."

Part of the difficulty of that task is simply the nature of football, in which players' skills are much more interdependent than in other sports. In baseball, a player's skills are largely isolated. He may have more or fewer runs batted in, depending on the players hitting before him, he may hit more or fewer homers, depending on his home park, but his performance for one team is largely the same as his performance for another. In pro football, that's not the case. A small, agile guard who excels in pulling and trapping can be an All-Pro–caliber player in one offense, but the same player can be a liability on another team built around a pile-driving straightforward running attack.

And while some of this is made apparent through dedicated film study, much of it isn't evident. With the advent of free agency, the roles of college player personnel and pro player personnel merged somewhat, and the bulging files of scouted college players moved directly to the pro personnel department, where they were augmented with scouting reports and other information. But the simple fact is that you can't monitor seventeen hundred far-flung players over the course of their pro careers the way you can isolate, test, and quiz a few hundred draft-eligible players who will gather at combines, sit for interviews, and show up for personal scouting days in the months before the draft.

"On a purely practical level, you don't know as much about the [pro] player as you do someone you draft," says one GM. "The odds of making a mistake are much greater, and you are rolling the dice every time."

In 1997, the Kansas City Chiefs went 13–3 before an early playoff exit. They seemed to lack only a major run-stopping, gap-eating defensive tackle. As the story goes, Chester McGlockton, the All-Pro tackle of the Raiders—whom the Chiefs owned in the nineties—stopped Kansas City coach Marty Schottenheimer after a game and told him he wanted to sign with the Chiefs.

So when McGlockton was signed as a free agent, hopes were high in Kansas City. One columnist predicted the team would go 16–0 the following year, and players were seriously talking about setting defensive records.

I'm reminded of the scene in the Dan Jenkins novel *Baja Oklahoma*, when a stunning young woman walks out of a bar and leaves a dazzled man staring. At the corner of the bar, though, Slick Henderson reminds him, "Somewhere, somebody's tired of her."

And so it is with NFL free agents.

Chemistry is a delicate thing, even in an NFL locker room. It's never as simple as plugging a good player into a hole. McGlockton didn't fit. And I can remember before the 1998 season, while I was still the Vikings' offensive coordinator and before one of our annual July scrimmages with the Chiefs, I was

34

on the field at River Falls, talking with Schottenheimer, who seemed less animated than usual.

At one point, he looked at me and said, "Brian, I'm worried. I don't like my team."

He couldn't have been more prescient. Picked by many to make a Super Bowl run, the Chiefs imploded during the season. Unbeknownst to anyone then, McGlockton had already gone to his last Pro Bowl. And late in that 1998 season, the Chiefs melted down in a Monday Night Football loss to Denver, suffering six personal fouls in an embarrassing display that earned the great Derrick Thomas a one-game suspension and led to the immediate release of Wayne Simmons, another free-agent signing. The chemistry wasn't right, and a few weeks after the season, Schottenheimer left after ten years with the Chiefs (a move he still regrets, by the way).

The league is full of stories of "must-have" players wooed by teams that were convinced they were just one player away from a championship. In 1994, the Cleveland Browns went 11–5 under Bill Belichick before losing in the divisional round of the playoffs to Pittsburgh. With Vinny Testaverde at quarterback, and a backfield that included Earnest Byner, Leroy Hoard, and Eric Metcalf, the Browns were convinced that they were one player away from the promised land. Art Modell always talked about "getting my coach what he needs," and in '94, what Bill Belichick thought he needed was Andre Rison, who had averaged about eighty catches, one thousand yards, and ten touchdowns a year in his first six seasons with the Falcons. "Bill was just convinced he was the key to winning a Super Bowl," says Modell. So the Browns signed Rison to a five-year, $17 million deal with a $5 million signing bonus . . . and went 5–11 the next season. That was a nightmare season for a lot of reasons—the Browns announced their move to Baltimore, the team suffered a long losing streak, Rison was mediocre (catching just forty-seven passes in an ineffectual year), and the season concluded with the team firing a future Hall of Fame coach, Belichick. Rison would end up with only eight total touchdowns in his remaining seven years in the league.

One of my most vivid memories of my early experiences with free agency was sitting down and talking with an offensive lineman who was coming off a Super Bowl performance and hitting the streets as a free agent. In a fit of honesty, he said, "I have my Super Bowl ring. Now all I want to do is get paid."

"You overpay in free agency," says one GM. "You eat up budget dollars, cap dollars, and you expend emotional assets. And the dance of trying to talk players into coming is so superficial, it's nonsensical."

By the twenty-first century, many teams had followed the lead of New England, which under Bill Belichick and vice president of player personnel Scott Pioli (who has since moved to Kansas City to become the Chiefs' general manager) went with a very no-nonsense approach to recruiting. Learning from his previous mistakes with Rison, Belichick grew more cautious when he became head coach of the Patriots. Rather than limos and fancy suites, visiting free agents get a room in the Residence Inn. Then they are taken to the Patriots nearby training complex, and eat a dinner of carryout pizza while having a chalk talk with Belichick and an assistant coach.

Some teams will still court players—Dan Snyder's private helicopter is always on call to close deals for the Redskins—but most teams have recognized that they want players who aren't swayed by the glitz anyway.

"Now if someone is coming in and asking about schools and neighborhoods, that's one thing," says a veteran GM. "I'll get in my car and drive him around, talk to him about districts, commutes, neighborhood. But if someone wants to be wined and dined, and go see the Céline Dion show, forget about it."

I'm not sure how many free agents are asking for Céline Dion tickets, but I get his point.

GMs and coaches were soon reminded of what they had intuitively understood all along—while some turnover was inevitable, teams were stronger when the core group stayed together. And while you could get away with one or two "attitude" players if you had a secure core of leadership in your locker room—take a look at Randy Moss's performance in 2007 in New England compared to his previous two years in Oakland—you had to remain constantly vigilant about how the pieces were going to fit together.

The advent of free agency worked a couple of ways. Players, making nearly 60 percent of the league's gross revenues, became partners in the truest sense of the word. There are still plenty of people who think all pro athletes are overpaid, and in the simplest terms, that's inarguable. But to the extent that the NFL is profitable, the players are justified in receiving a large share. "Paying the price" isn't just a slogan in pro football; the game clearly takes years off the lives of the men who play it, and to see these glorious athletes, so strong and seemingly indestructible in their prime, reduced to crippled shells in their forties and fifties is to understand what they have sacrificed to play the sport.

But the added investment on the part of teams meant that players were no longer living under indentured servitude. The savvier owners and GMs understood that in a world in which the average player was making nearly $2 million per year, it made sense to take care of that investment. And in a world in which players could play elsewhere if they chose, it made sense to retain them, rather than risk the stab in the dark of free agency.

The Ravens built a $31 million training facility that includes everything from a gourmet cafeteria to a clubhouse with arcade and video games. The idea, none too subtle but profoundly important nonetheless, was to create an environment that players would want to be in even when they weren't practicing. When the rest of the world seems fraught with danger, staying at home has its appeal.

When the present system was installed in 1993, it came with a rookie pool that would keep rookie salaries in line. But rookies have agents, and agents are paid to find ingenious ways around things like rookie pools. So in the very first year of the CBA, rookie contracts began circumventing the spirit of the rookie pool. Rick Mirer, the second pick taken in that draft, signed a rookie contract with fifty-nine different contingencies and team incentives. Each of the incentives was originally designated "not likely to be earned," which meant the bonuses wouldn't count against Mirer's cap number that rookie season. But the statistical probability was that at least some of the incentives would be earned, and they were, which allowed Mirer to circumvent his earning limit as a rookie. That contract went to a grievance hearing and the league and the Players Association settled on a limit of eight team incentives for any contract in the future. "Now all the contracts have eight incentives," said one league vice president. "We should have kept it at two."

The floodgates opened with voidable years. If you sign a five-year contract with a $10 million signing bonus, that bonus is prorated over the life of the contract, so it would count $2 million per year against the cap. Voidable contracts stipulated that if a player met certain incentives, the later years in his contract could be voided. In the above example, with a five-year deal that voided after three years, the prorated bonus for the last two years of the deal would accelerate into the fourth year of the contract, but in the meantime, the player would have still gotten more money than he was technically allowed under the rookie cap.

It wasn't just the rookie cap that was used in a different way than originally intended. Franchise designations, originally designed to keep a John Elway–type franchise player from leaving his team, evolved into a way for teams to nail down a different up-and-coming player each season. Players hated it, because even though the tag paid them a sum equivalent to the average of the top five salaries in the league at the position, it was only for a single year, and guaranteed none of the security and longevity that players understandably long for.

Then came the Steve Hutchinson deal. In 2006, Hutchinson was an All-Pro guard who had been given the "transition tag" by the Seahawks (the transition player designation is a sort of junior version of the franchise player designation; with the transition tag, you're obligated to pay him a salary equal to the average of the top ten at his position). The Vikings signed him to a $49 million, seven-year deal with a poison-pill provision stipulating that if at any time Hutchinson wasn't the highest-paid offensive lineman on the team, the entire contract would become guaranteed. After having designated Hutchinson as a transition player, the Seahawks had the right of first refusal on Hutchinson, but they knew they couldn't match that deal—left tackle Walter Jones was already making more than Hutchinson, and making Hutchinson's contract a guaranteed one would have made a shambles of the Seahawks' cap. Hutchinson thus signed with the Vikings.

Because of these manipulations, every contract has become

a thicket of incentive clauses, voidable years, likely-to-be-earned and unlikely-to-be-earned bonuses, and myriad other details. Fifteen years ago, the standard boilerplate NFL contract was used for virtually every deal, and only the biggest contracts had to be vetted by a lawyer. Today, most teams send every single contract through a line-by-line reading by a lawyer, because agents have learned how to find the loopholes in the 344-page NFL collective-bargaining agreement.

And that Pandora's box, once opened, won't shut. "We do it to ourselves," says one GM. "We let ourselves manipulate our own rules."

The GM has more power than in the past, simply because there are more ways to acquire players, and there is more player movement overall. Because of those elements, it's absolutely imperative that the GM and his head coach be on the same page. Ozzie and I wouldn't always agree on every single personnel decision, but when we didn't, we talked it out until one of us swayed the other. Neither of us wanted an owner, who by definition knew less about the situation than we did, to cast a tie-breaking vote. So if we disagreed, we discussed it until we were 2–0 for or against.

As a coach, you are looking for immediate help and a short-term return on your investment with a top draft choice, preferably at a position of need. From that standpoint, taking tight end Todd Heap and safety Ed Reed late in the first round of the 2001 and 2002 drafts didn't seem prudent at the time, since we had players like Shannon Sharpe and Rod Woodson on the team already and we had other, more pressing needs. But through the evaluations and back-and-forth scrimmaging that are a part of personnel decisions, we arrived at a consensus and made what obviously became a good set of selections.

The challenge facing the general manager, and by extension, the head coach, is at times paradoxical. They are judged on the performance of the team, and that performance is built around the concept of teamwork, the value of putting the greater good first. Yet together, the GM and head coach must make personnel evaluations that are diametrically opposed to that mind-set. Each year the process of building a team begins with the ultimate non-team-building act of analyzing players on the basis of market value. The market says player A is worth X amount of money. In order to keep him you might have to reduce the contract of player B—without insulting him. And, if you are to keep both players A and B, player C has to be released.

What compounds this problem is that the organization has to start making these plans and putting them into action before the end of the previous season. In order to take advantage of any cap room left in the present year, and to gain more cap room in future years, a team will offer certain players extensions. Some players and their agents are not capable of separating their current priorities and the business side of the industry. The last thing you want as a coach is for a key player to be "offended" by your initial offer for the future. On the other hand, when a team makes no offer at all, the same player can begin to question the team's loyalty to him, and to wonder whether he's in the team's plans at all. Not the sort of problem you want in the middle of a playoff run.

There are many moving targets: The salary cap goes up slightly each year, some players will be re-signed (and get huge bonuses), some players will be cut before their contract is up (and their prorated bonuses will then accelerate into the present year), other free agents will be signed (more bonuses). The upshot is that any action must take into account not just the present but also the implications for the future. When Ozzie or our capologist Pat Moriarity came in and tried to explain to me how a contract would affect the cap situation, and how it would amortize out, I would have to put my hands up and plead, "Just tell me who it is going to cost me. The numbers mean nothing to me unless I can attach actual bodies to the cost."

When the New York Giants were building the team that advanced to the Super Bowl in 2000, they did so with Michael Strahan at one defensive end and Chad Bratzke on the other side. Bratzke had been a fifth-round draft choice out of Eastern Washington, a rangy, high-motor guy who was better than most people expected, and perfectly complemented the wrecking-ball thrusts of Michael Strahan on the other side.

In 1998, Bratzke had a great season, with eleven sacks in the last year of his contract. During that season, his agent called Giants' GM Ernie Accorsi to open contract negotiations.

Accorsi rebuffed him instantly. "I can't talk to you," he said. Accorsi knew that Strahan's contract was coming up a year later, and that if he signed his star Bratzke, he couldn't afford his superstar Strahan.

"Well, at least give us an offer," said Bratzke's agent, "maybe we can give you a hometown discount."

"I can't even do that. It's killing me. I can't even make an offer."

Looking back, Accorsi wouldn't change his plan, but he sees the downside. "If I sign him, then I wouldn't have been able to keep Strahan. Without a cap, we're set at the ends for twelve years. That was gone. You had to discipline yourself. And until you realized how it affected you, you couldn't truly handle it. It batters you emotionally; it batters you competitively."

That's the perspective that the GM has to keep at all times.

The same thing happened in Baltimore. After linebacker

Adalius Thomas had a great season in 2006, we had to let him go to New England. Ozzie Newsome did it because he knew he had fellow linebacker Terrell Suggs coming up for free agency the following year, and he simply couldn't keep both. It was an excrutiating choice, not only because of the value a player has on the field, but in the case of Thomas, the value he had as an emotional leader in the locker room and in the community. The Patriots signed Thomas to a big deal, but after the injury-plagued season of 2007, the Ravens' defense was again among the best in the NFL in 2008. Ozzie had made the right call.

Jon Gruden still remembers how tormented he felt having to let safety John Lynch go after the 2002 season. "I am wearing a Super Bowl ring because of that guy," says Gruden. "You don't just cast someone like John Lynch aside and say, 'Okay, who's next?' This side of the business just sucks."

Sometimes, the call goes beyond a single player and into the system as a whole.

In 2001, after the Colts fell from consecutive playoff berths to a 6–10 record, Bill Polian told his head coach, Jim Mora, that he'd have to fire defensive coordinator Vic Fangio. Both men were accomplished in their field, and they respected each other, but with so much money allotted to the offense—Peyton Manning, Marvin Harrison, Edgerrin James—Polian didn't feel he could give Fangio the tools he needed to build the sort of defense Fangio wanted.

"As we were evolving," says Polian, "it became clear to me that we couldn't have the kind of offensive system we had and still use that defensive system we had, and still make it fit under the cap. We couldn't do it." Polian respected Mora and Fangio but knew, when they got "crosswise," as he puts it, that he had to fire them.

(Fangio remembers it differently. "He told us we'd have to

keep 'ham-and-egging it' on defense," he says. "Then in the year after we leave, they go get [Dwight] Freeney and [Robert] Mathis," who would go on to become All-Pro performers in the defenses of Mora's successor, Tony Dungy.)

The same thing happened in Baltimore, though the roles were reversed. The defense shone, year in and year out, while the offense struggled. I was criticized for it, because my reputation had been built coordinating offenses. And Ozzie Newsome took the heat as well. But the decision he had to make—and it was a wise one—was to keep the superior players on one of the league's best defenses and let the others go.

It is vital that the GM also understand the different type of pressure that is on his head coach. Having been a Hall of Fame player, a scout, and a coach, Ozzie knew what I was experiencing, good or bad. I always said, "With Ozzie's lack of ego and my exaggerated one, we balance each other out." The compensation for head coaches and general managers is disproportionate, with most established coaches making twice or even three times as much as general managers. But even that was not an issue for Ozzie. "We'll call that combat pay, Coach," he'd say. "Because we both know that if it doesn't go well, you're the one who is going to get hit first."

The combination of huge guaranteed signing bonuses for unproven first-round draft choices and rookies and the great unknown of signing free agents created, after a while, a surprising effect: It revived the emphasis on the draft.

"What we all came to realize is that free agency was high-risk, often inheriting someone else's problem, and you could never be sure you were getting quality," says one GM. "Consequently, you had to draft well. They had to play and they had to play quickly.

You couldn't miss with the first-round choice, of course, but you also had to get value in every round. You needed to have contributions—starters, backups, practice squad at least—from every one of your picks."

If you take a look at the most successful franchises of the past ten years—New England, Indianapolis, Pittsburgh, the New York Giants, Philadelphia—you'll find a consistently strong draft record.

"If you talk about a franchise that has maintained, it's been Pittsburgh," says Ozzie Newsome. "They have always survived through the draft and allowed guys to walk. If you're a good drafting football team, you've always got young guys who are ready to replace those guys. And it balances your books. You look at Indianapolis now—they can have six or seven marquee players, then they can draft players at a position you don't think is premium. And in a salary cap, you can have that draft class for four years. If you have three good draft classes, you've got 40 to 60 percent of your football team playing for their second contract. You got 'em as cheap as you could get 'em, and you got Pro Bowl players."

If that was all there was to the job, it would be challenge enough. But in the new world order, the myriad football decisions are only one piece of the puzzle.

"It all began to change in the mid-nineties," says one GM. "It wasn't just free agency. It was the explosion of media, the explosion of new stadiums, and that all worked together to make it a 24/7, fifty-two-weeks-a-year business."

Some GMs, like Ozzie Newsome in Baltimore, rarely leave the office. "I'm going to be here every day," he says, "and people have to get used to that." Others travel only with the forbearance of their staff. The Colts' company plane takes Bill Polian to two games a week throughout the college football season, on Thursday nights and again on Saturdays.

When I first got to Baltimore, the constant presence of a GM took some getting used to. In Minnesota, Frank Gilliam was the GM and was constantly on the road looking at college players. This was the structure I was familiar with and early on, I questioned why Ozzie never went out to look at players. It didn't take long for me to recognize the value of Ozzie's staying at home. He was at every practice, allowing him to critique the progress of every player, young and old, and where they fit into the needs of the team. When scouts came off the road and expressed frustration that "their" young draft choice was not being used more, Ozzie was that creditable source who could give them the reason, having seen the player every day and knowing exactly where he was in his development. Had the scouts just heard the same reasoning from me they might have dismissed it as the coach's reliance on veteran players or his inability to develop the talent.

In addition, Ozzie could see in practice what the game plan was and how we planned on beating our opponent. Then when things didn't go well I didn't have to try to explain, after the fact, what had happened. He had seen the practices and understood that, even if it didn't work, there was a plan and it had been practiced properly.

There were other competitive reasons for the new generation of GMs to stay close to home. The 1990s and 2000s saw a stadium-building boom in the league, and new stadiums meant more signage to sell, more luxury boxes to sell, more sponsorship agreements to be struck, and many more meetings with people who sell and who buy all of those premiums.

And then there are the agents, always the agents. You have

to be exceptionally thick-skinned and secure in your position to be a successful GM in today's whirlwind of media, money, and headline-hungry agents. The GM has to maintain a good working relationship with people he quite frankly doesn't much care for. They are constantly contacting him during the season to voice the complaints and demands of their clients, and can become arrogant and condescending when they have the upper hand in a negotiation, then friendly and conciliatory when the shoe is on the other foot.

Once, after Ozzie had taken the time to explain to an agent that his demands, though reasonable, would cripple the team around the player we were discussing, the agent's response was, "That's not my problem. Once my client gets his money, how you do as an organization and a team is of no interest to me."

I always admired Ozzie's approach to dealing with agents, and his ability to take his own ego out of the process. "You just have to make sure they get their win," he told me once. "You always do what is best for the organization, but if you can do it in a way that can make the agent look good, then everyone wins. All I want is the player. I don't care who gets the credit." Too often GMs and agents get into a battle of wills in which neither feels he can give any ground. The zero-sum approach, in which the agent gets the better of the team, or vice versa, is a poor, unsustainable business practice that is driven by ego rather than economics.

With all that, it's no wonder the modern GMs tend to stay in the office.

"If you're a general manager, you need to be there to protect your family," says one longtime club executive. "And that, to me, means the team that's in the building. The best GMs are the ones who can multitask. They'll be out at practice, watching, paying attention, but also thinking about how to solve a cap problem, or what to do with a player who keeps getting in trouble off the field."

And then there's the nearly infinite echo chamber that is the modern media. Around the same time that the job was changing because of the salary cap and free agency, there were other variables coming into play that further complicated the sport.

On one hand was the explosion of talk radio, digital cable, and the internet, all of which saw the expansion of sports content. This may have affected football more than other sports, because there's more space between games in football, more time to be filled up with speculation and criticism. Make a horrendous mistake in baseball, and it's the top of the news until the following night's game. Make a horrendous mistake in football and you hear about it and see it replayed for a week.

Hand in hand with the sport's growing popularity and the dawn of the internet age came the rise in popularity of fantasy football. Suddenly, average to serious sports fans had a much greater appreciation for the challenges faced by general managers, to say nothing of many more opinions on the moves they made.

This confluence of events cast a much harsher light on the role of the general manager, who could no longer sit in the background unaffected by the media, as he might have in the past. Now the media were right up in his face. And if he was under pressure for a team's disappointing performance, it could be relentless.

"My family always tried to keep a sense of humor about it and keep it in the proper prospective," says Matt Millen, who was fired by the Lions in the middle of the 2008 season. "I knew we were okay when I came home on Christmas [in 2007] after they had put the tree up, and on the top was a snow angel holding a sign saying, 'Fire Millen.'"

After his largely successful twenty-year run in which the

Chiefs experienced a renaissance and became a perennial play-off team for much of the nineties, Carl Peterson took the brunt of the criticism for Kansas City's poor performance since 2003. When Peterson announced his resignation in December 2008, the *Kansas City Star* ran a six-column headline above the fold of its front page, reading "The reign is over." That sort of attention didn't exist a generation ago.

And the need to weather that stress and constant criticism calls for a more resilient psychological makeup. You don't have to be media-friendly, necessarily, but you certainly have to be media-resilient. Polian has a reputation as a prickly perfectionist, with an explosive temper. But he communicates well with others and has the presence for the job. Tony Dungy never had a radio show in Indianapolis, but Polian did. He didn't like it, but the organization needed to have someone to interact with the public, serve as a sounding board, field the angry calls, and take the heat. Polian can deliver as well.

You would be hard pressed to find two people whose personalities and communication styles are more different than Bill Polian and Ozzie Newsome. However, the reason they are both so successful is they have a great capacity to listen and filter the information they are getting. "Bill can beat you up pretty good when you want to present your case for a player," says Dungy. "But you know he is listening and taking in every important fact in order to help him make a decision."

I have sat through countless personnel, organizational, and league meetings with Ozzie. He seldom says anything, and frankly, at times seems to be not paying attention at all. Then, the next day, week, or month, in some discussion about the subjects or players that had been discussed, he will recall the exact context and make the perfect connection between what was discussed earlier and what has to be decided now.

As I watched Ozzie on draft day looking up at our board with five hundred plus names on it, I would marvel at his capacity to absorb it all and draw on whatever he needed at that instant. He reminded me of the John Nash character played by Russell Crowe, looking at the chalkboard in the movie *A Beautiful Mind*, with all the equations and information coming to life before his eyes. He saw things the rest of us couldn't see—facts within patterns, and patterns within facts—or at least couldn't see all at once.

The complexity of the job is endless. There isn't a GM in football who's ever truly off work. You can say you're going on vacation, or taking a few days at the beach house. But if something goes wrong, you will get called and you'll need to respond.

"When I come in each morning, I have no idea what I'm going to have waiting for me," says Newsome. "People think I'm just sitting here and evaluating talent. But there's going to be a trainer with a medical report, and now we've got to pick up someone, or it's a wife of a player calling me with a problem. This is an hour-by-hour job. It's talking to some of these rookies who don't understand how important it is to get to work on time."

What Polian, Newsome, Pioli, and others who have succeeded in the position share is a background in personnel, a vital component of the job in the modern age. To try to take the job without that background, or else a very trusted, very adept personnel man as your sidekick, is to court disaster.

Matt Millen was part of four Super Bowl teams during his playing career, and worked ten years as a color commentator. But in the eight years he served as a GM in Detroit, his Lions were 31–95. "I have known Matt for twenty years and like him a great deal," says one NFL scout. "His hiring said to me that some ownership does not truly value what we do, nor do they appreciate how difficult this job is. After spending years and years on the road to every Podunk College in America, learning to identify and quantify the talent it takes to win in this league, then to see a guy with literally no background or experience whatsoever, and think that he could just step into that responsibility, well it's insulting." Of course, a background in personnel doesn't guarantee success. There have been personnel people elevated to jobs who couldn't handle the responsibilities of frequent contact and dealing with people throughout the organization. They either try to handle it all and lose focus, or they treat the rest of the building as the enemy, and lose support. It's a tricky balancing act.

The GM has to answer for every decision about the team that goes on the field. Who to hire as a coach? Who to draft? Who to sign? Probably a hundred player contracts a year, and probably twenty more coaching and staff contracts. Endless hours of game film in a buildup to the draft. Twelve-hour days, long meetings around conference tables, in which a committee tries to reconcile the impossible. Inevitably, the player with the higher upside also has the greater negatives. And a decision has to be made: Can it be managed? Can we control it?

A general manager assembles this complex machine. From the day after the end of his team's season, he's in charge, making a thousand decisions involving coaching, players, drafts, free-agent signings, support staff, sponsorships, media management. He is atop a magnificent construction, with hundreds of variables, all of which are interconnected in one way or another.

And then, when the games begin on the first weekend after Labor Day—Kickoff Weekend, as the NFL has taken to calling it—it is more or less out of his hands. And he suffers.

"There isn't a job in professional sports," says Ernie Accorsi, "with more pressure and less control. It's agonizing."

THE ILLUSION
OF CONTROL

In the summer of 1977, I was cut by the San Francisco 49ers—who explained to me in no uncertain terms that I didn't have a career as a pro football player (I lacked both the speed and the athleticism needed for the tight end position)—and returned to my hometown of Redlands, California. I had wanted to coach football for nearly as long as I had wanted to play the game, so I knew what to do next.

There were two legendary coaches in Redlands. Frank Serrao coached the college team at Redlands University, an NAIA school, and Paul Womack was the coach at Redlands High School, where I had played. When I returned, Serrao offered me a volunteer position to coach the wide receivers, and Womack let me serve as his assistant with the high school team. I would go to the high school practice from two to four o'clock, then head over to the university (where the Los Angeles Rams used to hold their training camps) for the college practice. Though I would occasionally catch myself barking one school's terminology at another school's practice, it was one of the most rewarding years I have ever spent in coaching.

From the first day you put a whistle around your neck and trot out on a football field without a helmet, trying to teach a group of not-much-younger men the fundamentals of what you were doing just a year or two earlier, you start thinking about what it will be like when you get to be a head coach. Most coaches start their career shortly after college, meaning that by the time they work their way up from an assistant's job to a coordinator's job to a head coaching job, it's something they've been pointing to for two decades or more.

You watch the men whom you work under. I was fortunate to have some of the best. The great Bill Walsh in San Francisco. Doug Scovil, a sharp, innovative thinker at San Diego State. Denny Green, smart, sensitive to his players, solid as a rock at Stanford and in Minnesota with the Vikings. You learn things, and you file them away, creating a mental composite of how you might be wiser, more prepared, more proficient. The way this coach handles two-a-days, or the way that one manages the clock. This one's a Neanderthal to his players, but he treats his assistants well. And you decide that when you get to be a head coach, it will be different.

Tony Dungy and Bill Cowher vowed, during their days on Marty Schottenheimer's staff in Kansas City, that they would never sleep in their offices, and when they became head coaches, they worked to create an environment in which their assistants didn't have to. My vow during my years as an assistant was more technological. I'd seen smart coaches who were irrationally dismissive, even frightened, about the advent of computers, and I was determined to use computers more efficiently in any staff I led.

Like a lot of first-time head coaches, I thought I was ready for the pressure and the responsibility. I thought I wouldn't be surprised by all the trappings that came with the position. And then, just days after getting hired by the Ravens in January 1999, I found out different.

I had heard before taking the job that, like it or not, head coaches were the face of a franchise. It didn't matter if you had a visible owner, or an All-Pro quarterback. The coach set the tone for the team, and the city responded to how the coach handled the pressure. I recognized this in theory. But I didn't really *understand* it.

After I was hired by the Ravens, I immediately headed down to the Senior Bowl in Alabama, then took a week to return to Minnesota and gather up my things and quickly prepare for the move. I flew back to Baltimore with my wife, Kim, and was just driving into downtown Baltimore when I saw something unexpected from the beltway.

A huge billboard. With my face, however many stories high. And one word: BILLICK.

My first thought was that I am entirely too ugly to have my face blown up that big. The second thought was that there was little doubt what the expectations were going to be. Beside me in the car, Kim just laughed.

Each NFL coach knows that when the first whistle blows to begin your very first training camp practice, the job is truly 24/7 until the gun ending your last game of the season, ideally in early February at the Super Bowl. Everyone at some point alludes to his or her job as dominating his or her life, or occupying almost every waking minute, but I know of few people in any other profession who work from late July to January without a single day off. Even in the military soldiers get R & R after a couple of months. Yet in this relentless, remorseless schedule—while always fearful that your opponent is at this very instant working harder to gain some precious edge over you—each coach has to find a rhythm that fits his personality.

The typical workweek is daunting. You get home Sunday evening after a home game, or late, late Sunday night after a road game. Physically and emotionally drained, you check some of the Sunday night TV game, find out how your friends and foes are doing around the league, then drift off to sleep.

Monday morning it starts, with coaches in the office by eight o'clock. Everybody is watching and grading film from the previous day's game, then convening to compare notes. (Coaches have called it "film" for decades, even though it was videotape for much of that time, and is now digital video on a computer. It's all film to us.) There's a short meeting with the team, a longer meeting among the staff, and then it's time to prepare for the next opponent. The quality-control coaches will have been up most of the night making cut-ups for the next game, film collages of the opposing team in various situations—first and ten, second and long, second and short, third and short, third and medium, third and long. The head coach will be going over game films in full, to get some sense of the rhythm of the other team's offense. You leave around 10:00 P.M., and the rest of the staff follows shortly thereafter. (The head coach can tell the staff to leave whenever they're done, but in fact nobody leaves before the head coach.)

Tuesday morning, most coaches are in the office by six o'clock. It is the quintessential workday. Tuesday is an off-day for players, so coaches are working together on coming up with the game plan. You will often be in the office for sixteen hours on this day, and if you get done by midnight, it's been a good day. You're getting into the guts of the game plan, working up the ready list of plays, and figuring out what to focus on during the following day's practice. The last laborious task of the night is the cards—a set of play diagrams that need to be practiced by the offense and the defense. This is a painstaking process and it has to be done right, and many assistants are in the office well past midnight.

The next day is the same thing: 6:00 A.M. arrival, more film, more game-planning, more ready lists, plus meetings and practice. It is the beginning of putting in the game plan and walking through the plays to be run. After the players leave, coaches go back to work: third down, red zone, special situations. It's another sixteen-hour day.

Thursday is another 6:00 A.M. arrival, and the completion of the game plan. We practice early, and you send your coaches home by 7:00 P.M., so they can reacquaint themselves with the strangers in their family. Friday is another 6:00 A.M. arrival, but ideally only a ten- or eleven-hour day, since there is little more that can be done in the way of game-planning or practicing (which isn't to say you won't bring work home with you).

On Saturday, you're in by 8:00 A.M. for the final walk-through and then the flight out of town or, in the event of a home game, a brief break before everyone has to report to the hotel by 6:00 P.M. Home or away, most teams stay together in a hotel near the stadium. Home or away, team and unit meetings are at 9:00 P.M. By then, we know what we're going to do, and we usually know who we'll do it with. There may be a few last-minute adjustments, based on weather, or a player tweaking himself in warm-ups, but for the most part, it's all taken care of by Saturday night.

On Sunday, we play football.

It's an exhausting game, emotionally draining, physically damaging to players, and physically demanding of coaches. Coaches can only maintain their pace if they exercise—treadmill, lifting, racquetball, whatever works—four or five days a week. Coffee is brewed by 5:30 A.M., and Diet Cokes seem to multiply in offices during the day. Yet there are days where you nod off while watching game film, days when you ask your secretary to hold all calls for twenty minutes, close the door, and take a nap that feels like a matter of life and death. You wake, groggy, still fighting cobwebs, but refreshed. And it's worth it. If you're barking at your players, punchy, or unprepared, the teaching experience is compromised. And players can tell when you've prepared and when you're faking it.

Authentic energy and drive are what count. Herm Edwards emphasized that point during the 2008 season when the Kansas City Chiefs made the organizational choice to totally rebuild the team and put one of the youngest teams ever in the league on the field. "These young guys don't know how they are supposed to act in the NFL," says Edwards, who knew then that the sacrifice he was making might well cost him his job. (It did.) "You have to be upbeat and energetic, and it can't just be an act. They will see through that in a minute."

Now, realize: *Everyone* works hard. We're grinders by nature. And yet as a group we still tend to exaggerate because we're so insecure. It's madness, but we're all susceptible. When *Sports Illustrated*'s Peter King was talking with me about the fabled early hour that Jon Gruden reportedly gets to the office, he asked when I get in. "A half hour before whatever time Gruden lies about getting in," I said. It's always been thus: Back in the sixties, George Allen, coming into the office one morning, was greeted by his secretary informing him he had Vince Lombardi waiting on the phone. "Tell him you got me out of a meeting," Allen said.

Coaches convince themselves that if they work longer, or stay up later, they are somehow outworking their opponent.

It doesn't often happen. The words of fabled basketball coach John Wooden come to mind: "Don't mistake activity for productivity."

Yet this collective fear feeds on itself throughout the staff. Each season begins with teams talking about working smarter and more efficiently. And by December, most of the league is sleeping in their office a few nights a week. You might think that winning breeds the obsession, but it's there in any case. Losing only adds more urgency. There are many coaches in this league, when faced with failure, who learn only one lesson: I have to work harder. In December 2008, one losing team's first meeting started at four-thirty in the morning. Don't be late.

All of that work builds toward the game-day experience, which can be transformative in its own right. I knew one college coach who couldn't wear anything but shirtsleeves on game days, even in subfreezing weather, because he was so keyed up during games, he would overheat.

During one season, I started to experience heart palpitations during the games. I thought to myself more than once, "My God, I am having a heart attack doing this job." When I told our team physician, Andy Tucker, about the symptoms, he did all the relevant testing (EKG, stress test, echocardiogram, and so forth) and found nothing alarming. So Andy decided to shadow me on game days. After a couple of observations, he asked me how much coffee I typically drank during the week. I'm not a big coffee drinker, and told him I would have one or two cups in the morning as I went to work. On Sundays before the game, though, I was changing my caffeine intake. I would have a cup when I got up, another reading the paper, one during breakfast, and a fourth on my walk to the stadium. Andy told me, "You're drinking enough coffee that after the game, you're not only not tired, you could probably start vacuuming the garage."

Of course, the most difficult part of this profession is the strain it puts on our families. Many families have to deal with the ups and downs of a profession, the constant moving and uprooting, and the time away from your wife and children. But few jobs do it in such a public forum. I started out thinking I would never talk about work at home, thus saving my family from the pressures of the industry. All that did was leave them to reading the papers and listening to the radio to learn what was going on, and trying to figure out why their dad was being called the village idiot this week.

Dick Vermeil was able to keep a much better perspective about games as his career wore on, but even in his later years, the losses hurt. "When I walked into my office Sunday and saw my wife and saw my coaching staff's wives, I'll tell you, whew, it ain't worth it," he said in 2002, after his Chiefs squandered a big lead to lose a close game. "You can't do it too long. Because you are not the only one who suffers. You're not the only one that dies, but you know that this is your responsibility. And you're conditioned—you've coached yourself how to handle it. But the other parts of your life, they aren't coached."

In 1997, when I was the offensive coordinator for the Minnesota Vikings, we were under a great deal of pressure for our jobs. Even though we had been in the playoffs every year but one while I was there, we had yet to win a playoff game, and the rumors had begun. If we did not beat the New York Giants in the first round of the playoffs, it was being whispered, we were all gone. On Thursday night before the game, I got home early enough to put my then-eight-year-old daughter Keegan to bed. As we were talking about her week she paused as though she had a question, but could not quite get it out. After I prodded her a little, she asked, "Daddy, if we lose to the Giants this week do I have to leave my school and my friends?"

We subsequently beat the Giants in the Meadowlands on a fourteen-point comeback in the fourth quarter, so my daughter did not have to leave her friends after all. At least not until the next year, when I would leave to become the head coach for the Ravens.

When you take a job in coaching you take an unofficial oath that you understand the pressures of the game, and that is just the price you pay to be working in a profession you love. Your families, however, aren't given an option and have to take on the burdens of the profession whether they want to or not.

But I'm lucky. I've been happily married to the same woman for twenty-nine years. You see others who are less fortunate, and whose lives at home either deteriorate into unmanageability or are cut off altogether. You see the carnage of the life and its excesses, its abuses and follies, from alcoholism, to infidelity, to fractured marriages and broken families. One of the men who made the game more civil for players and coaches alike, Bill Walsh, had his own demons, and it didn't take very long to figure out what they were. In David Harris's biography of Walsh, *The Genius,* he chronicles the difficulties Walsh had reconciling his public persona with his private life, and in the numerous extramarital affairs that led to so much family anguish. I knew Bill to be devoted to his wife, Geri, and their children, yet Bill fell victim to the emotional outlet he felt he needed away from home to somehow balance the demands of his job.

Somehow a coach has to navigate the schedule and its pitfalls, the staggering amount of study, the mass of distractions and organizational challenges, the crises with players and coaches, and balance all these elements in such a way that he can stay on top of the job. And be himself while doing so.

When the demands of the job made it appear that I loved it more than my family, I would frequently remind them that the job was not more important than they were, only less forgiving.

You have to know a lot about football strategy and tactics to succeed as a head coach, but that's not the main requirement. The main requirement is understanding and being able to motivate players. This is not a board game.

And to understand players is to understand the power of money. One of the lessons that hits you full force very quickly as an NFL coach is that players can become preoccupied to the point of obsession about money. Assistant coaches are aware of the issue, but not in the same way as a head coach, who comes to understand the way that money insinuates itself into the essence of the game. We don't talk about this with our players, but it's always there, spurring us all on, and at times pushing us apart.

The root cause of many of the conflicts between players and coaches in the NFL can be found in a simple dichotomy: Players are driven and judged primarily by individual performances; head coaches are judged almost exclusively by the single criterion of winning. To understand those different priorities is to understand much of the difficulty of the modern game.

Players are keenly aware that their shelf life is ridiculously short. The average NFL career lasts just three and a half seasons. Even successful careers rarely last more than ten years. Players are very myopic about maximizing their income during their career, a journey made all the more perilous by the fact that most of their contracts are not guaranteed, and any career can end on a single play. The first contract a player signs is largely a product of draft position; third contracts rarely can be counted on, except for truly exceptional players. So much of the focus in the NFL is about setting yourself up for a second-contract windfall.

None of the above should suggest that winning is not important to players; in a vast majority of cases it is. It's just that winning is not the prime directive of their mission statement in the way it is for coaches. Players are surrounded by people—wives, friends, agent, family members—urging them to grab the money while they can and look out for themselves first, and the reality is that often what determines the size of their next contract is not the team's won-loss record but their own individual statistics.

So the rookie will tell you he just wants to help his team win. In fact he just wants to make the team. Once he has done so, he wants to earn his playing time. Once he's in the lineup, he often becomes preoccupied with touches, sacks, carries, or whatever benchmark he needs to gain recognition for his next contract.

In 2006, the Ravens bounced back from a disappointing season and won the AFC North Division title with a franchise-record mark of 13–3. Yet wide receiver Derrick Mason, as good a player as I have ever had, and as hard a worker, was incensed for much of the season, as it became increasingly clear that he would not approach the ninety catches that he had averaged over the three previous seasons. Of course, our team was able to go 13–3 in large part because of the play of other players, like Todd Heap and Demetrius Williams, who offered quarterback Steve McNair viable options to Mason that Raven quarterbacks hadn't had in the past. The other receivers offered the perfect balance to the skills that Derrick brought to the field, and that explosive offensive variety was part of the reason we were so successful, just as it was part of the reason that Derrick didn't get as many "touches." A year later, the team fell to 5–11, due in large part to injures to Heap and Williams. Meanwhile, Mason returned to his ninety-catch benchmark and acted happy as a clam.

Even assistant coaches can be guilty of this self-interest. Yes, they are more susceptible to the consequences of winning and losing as a team, but the individual statistical indicators of their effectiveness (such as team offensive and defensive rankings) may allow them to, at least, survive the consequences of team failures or, at best, garner the attention that might elevate them to a head-coaching position.

Only the head coach is held accountable for the bottom line of wins and losses. This is why coaches often take losing so much more to heart and take so long into the week to shed the desperation of the last loss. It was as much for himself as for his players that Marty Schottenheimer instituted his famous "midnight rule," counseling the team to suffer over a loss only until midnight, and then force themselves to turn their attention to the next opponent.

Occasionally, a coach will have the fortune of finding a player, or better yet, two or three players, who have made all the Pro Bowls and all the money they need, but are still driven by the quest for that one elusive, career-completing Super Bowl ring. In our 2000 Super Bowl season, players like future Hall of Fame defensive back Rod Woodson, quarterback Trent Dilfer, and defensive linemen Tony Siragusa and Rob Burnett all knew this was likely their last, best chance at a title. That breeds a constructive mentality that is felt throughout the team. But it is rare.

A head coach finds out soon enough that it's not just the players who are important. There are more than one hundred other employees who take their lead from the attitude of the coaching staff and the team, as well as a city full of fans and a national (and sometimes even worldwide) network of diehard supporters, for whom the team is not merely a rooting interest but a psychic touchstone.

"That was one of the most stark lessons I had to learn early in my head coaching career, how the players, coaches, even the owners and the fans and media will take their cues from you," says Dick Vermeil. "As people know, I am a very emotional guy, and I don't think I appreciated how much people based their emotional perspective on how I was acting. We lost eight in a row in my first year back in St. Louis and the whole building was waiting to see how I was going to react each Monday I walked in that door."

Kevin Byrne, the outstanding vice president of communications for the Baltimore Ravens and longtime veteran of the NFL wars, has long contended that the fans need to see the coach upset after a game to validate their own emotional attachment to the team. In short, it helps serious fans to see how much the coach cares. The problem comes when you take that impulse one step too far in this digital age, and find a brief flare-up memorialized for weeks, even years.

Everyone wants accountability, but not necessarily beginning with him- or herself. There were two messages that had to be delivered to the Ravens, both on and off the field. With any organization, there is a tendency to believe that as long as your department is doing well, you're doing fine. I was joining an organization that by all accounts was better run and more ably staffed than the one I had just left. Art Modell had the ability to identify and attract the best people, from Ozzie Newsome to Kevin Byrne, and the list went on and on. But the team I had just left, the Minnesota Vikings, had gone 15–1, while the Ravens had yet to have a winning season and had just come off a 6–10 season. The message I needed to deliver was that everyone in the building was going to be judged by the team's record. As I learned a long time ago from my mentor Denny Green, "You are who you are and your record is what it is."

Among the first meetings I had in Baltimore was a talk with the team's nonfootball employees, many of whom were renowned in their field, from Byrne's award-winning media relations department to Bill Tessendorf's excellent training staff to the crack operations director, Bob Eller. "I was just in Minnesota," I told the assembled staff, "and this place clearly is stronger in a lot of ways. But the team I left was 15–1, and this team is 6–10. So, even if you have sold out the stadium, gotten awards for your publications and releases, and had the best training staff in the league, the fact is that, for right now, you're a 6–10 training staff, and a 6–10 media relations department, and a 6–10 operations crew. You cannot separate the two. We're all in this together."

Next, the players needed to know that the fact that fifteen good men had been let go as the Ravens' coaching staff did not mean all our problems had left the building.

The owner needs to know what to expect, as does everyone else in the organization, all the way down to the guy with the lowliest job. "You have to find a way to connect with everyone in the building," says Vermeil. "You have to try to get them to understand their role, within the overall organization, to building a winning atmosphere."

There's obviously a line between getting everyone to buy into the program on one hand, and trying to micromanage everyone's jobs on the other hand. A lot of good coaches have been susceptible to the temptation to do the latter. During his two-year stint as the head coach in Kansas City, Gunther Cunningham took to checking the shampoo dispensers in the team showers. I've seen other coaches fall into the same trap. I've also known coaches who became so obsessed with what one columnist or one talk-show host says about them that they lose all sense of proportion. There is only so much you can control.

Bill Walsh identified the perspective you have to maintain with the players and the people in your organization in our book *Finding the Winning Edge*: "This balancing of micro and macro management is not unlike appreciating a work of art. If you stand too close to the piece you may be able to appreciate the fine detail and texture of the material, but you do so at the risk of being so close that you cannot keep the entire scope of the work in proper perspective. If you stand too far back you may have a better view of the 'Big Picture' but you risk losing the appreciation of the attention to detail and the quality of the work."

Tony Dungy and I learned under Denny Green that another way to maintain a constant interaction between the head coach and his players was to run the offensive and defensive scout teams in practice. Doing so establishes a daily interaction with virtually every member of the squad. That in turn creates a truly open-door policy with the players; they are more willing to go to the head coach and address an issue because they have already interacted with him during the day in a more informal setting. It also gives the players a tangible way of seeing the head coach actively involved in the preparation for the next opponent.

But whatever you do, you have to adjust to the visibility.

In my first year as the Ravens' coach we traveled down to Atlanta to take on the same Falcons team that had upset the Vikings the previous year in Minnesota to knock us out of the Super Bowl. It was a thrilling 19–13 overtime win for the Ravens and me. As is my usual routine, when I had satisfied all my obligations with the media, my staff, and the trainers, I got on the bus and called my eighty-year-old mother. She has always been my biggest fan and avidly followed whatever team I was with. No matter what the outcome of the game I could always be assured I was going to get a warm reception and a "you did great" from her.

This was the first time she'd seen me as a head coach on TV. I called expecting the usual congratulatory message, and instead I was greeted with a cool response. I could tell she was aggravated. It wasn't long before she blurted, "Do you think you could possibly say the work 'fuck' one more time on national television?!"

I had never heard my mother use that term in her life, so I knew I was in serious trouble. "I don't want to ever see that again," she admonished.

Lesson learned. When you're a head coach, everybody's watching. Including your own mother.

So there is the challenge of running an organization. Many who are up to it are less adept at dealing with the emotional challenge. I don't care who you are or at what level you played the game, there's something consuming about the first time you lead your team out onto the field. Part of the weight is the responsibility that one naturally feels, and that never really goes away. Think of the human effort involved: with fifty-three players, a coaching staff of around twenty, and at least as many support staff for the training, support, and communications, it's not uncommon that a team puts five thousand man-hours of preparation into a week's work for a single game.

Losing a single game in the NFL has the same competitive weight as a ten-game losing skid in baseball, or a five-game losing streak in the NBA. Consequently, each week feels like an absolute must-win. I am always asked, usually beginning in November, if the current game is a "must win." I always point out that a game in September has as much bearing on the final standings and on whether you are going to make the playoffs as a game in November or December does. The latter are just more easily identified as such.

One of the best things a coach can do is find a set time to get away from the game. I learned a great deal from Denny Green, but none of the lessons was more lasting than what he taught me about keeping perspective.

Denny is an avid fisherman, and in Minnesota we were never very far from some form of fishing. During the season, Denny would reward himself on Mondays—though only after wins—with a couple of hours of fishing before going in to work. This was a way of finding peace away from the game that helped preserve his sanity during the season.

The longer you last as a head coach the more you have to find the middle ground between the incredible mood swings caused by winning and losing. What tends to happen is that the wins become less important than the losses, and the effect of the wins becomes more short-lived. Some of this is due to the pressure imposed by the media and fans and the constant second-guessing. In order to avoid the emotional drain of the up and down mood swings, you find a middle where you can avoid getting either too excited or too depressed.

Yet the effects of losing still seep through, and wound. After a seventeen-year head coaching career in the NFL, the last ten in Seattle, Mike Holmgren stepped down in December 2008. "The lows just become too devastating, while the highs were short-lived," he said. "It is hard to keep the proper balance. In my case I felt I just needed to step away to regain the proper balance."

That idea that there's a magic ten-year limit on how long a coach can effectively communicate with the same team has some adherents. Bill Walsh was a firm believer in that idea. "The familiarity with the players, the others in the organization, even the media and fans just makes it problematic in going forward together," he said.

His protégé Mike Holmgren disagrees. "Each situation is different. The concept is sound, I just don't know if you can put a specific timetable on it."

It's probably not a coincidence that one of the people who seemed to need coaching the least was also among those most temperamentally suited for longevity. I coached with Tony Dungy for four years in Minnesota and against him for many years when he was turning the Colts into a perennial power, and he was as intense a competitor as there was in the league.

But for Tony it has always been about a bigger picture.

"I love to compete and love coaching, and being around these players. But there comes a point in your life where you have to ask, 'Should I be doing something else?' Is there another challenge, or another purpose I should be focusing on?"

After the 2008 season, Tony decided it was time for another challenge. Most coaches are hard-pressed to find something that will engage them as fully as coaching.

Focus.

That is hardest thing about the job. There are so many moving parts, and for them all to run well, you can't get bedeviled by one detail or another. In the end, being a head coach is about leadership, decision-making, and time management. And if you can't master the third, it will affect your success with the first two.

There is no place where the ability to narrowly focus on the task at hand is more overrated than during halftime of an NFL football game. People have long made too big a deal about the adjustments, or lack thereof, made by coaches and teams during halftime. The fact of the matter is that by the time everyone gets to the locker room, makes a run to the bathroom, and then gets back together to figure out what has just happened, you have precious little time to implement sweeping changes or give some grandiose pep talk.

In our 2000 championship season, there was no bigger game than the second, against divisional rival Jacksonville. The franchise had never beaten the Jaguars, and in the home opener, we made several errors and generally looked terrible in the first half, falling behind by seventeen points.

Halftime was not a time for ranting or raving. What adjustment were we going to make? Down by seventeen against a team that had owned us, I felt that talking about *winning* the game would have been the very definition of arrogance. I did tell the players that "win or lose—and truly winning or losing is insignificant—it is how we conduct ourselves in the second half that is going to determine what kind of team we are." The players took the challenge and came back to win on a last-minute touchdown pass from Tony Banks to Shannon Sharpe for an incredible 39–36 win.

With the advent of new technology, in particular the portability of digital technology for film review, access to research data has become both easier and more problematic. The easy access to all this information was supposed to save us time and energy, and Denny Green once calculated that it saved everyone on his staff up to two hours a day. Of course, Green didn't follow up on that savings by sending his staff home two hours earlier. All it meant was that they could use that extra time engaging in finer-grained preparations for their (already specialized) game-planning responsibilities.

Coaches seem to live by Parkinson's Law, which states that "work expands so as to fill the time available for its completion." My wife always used to ask about the preparation cycle when we had a Thursday night game. She would invariably ask, "Well, if you can get your work done between a Sunday and a Thursday, why does it take from Sunday to Sunday during a normal week?" The answer, though never satisfying her question, was always the same: "Because it does."

The overwhelming time crunch a coach works under was made even clearer to me when I took over the duties of offensive coordinator in the 2006 season. After a disappointing 6–10 season in 2005, we acquired quarterback Steve McNair from the Tennessee Titans and had high expectations going into the 2006 season. We started 4–2 on the year but offensively we were not performing at the level I thought we were capable of, and the players knew it. I felt I needed to take control of the situation and fired my offensive coordinator, Jim Fassel. Jim was a longtime successful coordinator and former Giants head coach whom I had faced in Super Bowl XXXV. He was also a longtime friend, and making the change was particularly tough, personally and professionally.

I knew that taking over the play calling, something I had not done since my first year with the Ravens six years earlier, was going to be a daunting task, in terms of both energy and time. I had always believed that the duties of the head coach had grown to the point that it was impossible to do both. As a former longtime offensive coordinator I knew the job was all-consuming. There are several coaches who have done both, and very well. But the number has dwindled as the game has grown more complex in the twenty-first century, and few coaches try to do both for any length of time.

In 2008, six teams had head coaches who also served as the primary play caller on offense. Only one went to the playoffs— San Diego at 8–8. I am not saying that the teams that have coaches that do both are unsuccessful because of the practice, but for me the idea that you can effectively do both is disrespectful to both positions. When you are an offensive coordinator trying to make a name for yourself in the profession, there is just not enough time in the day to do everything you need to. Your hours are as long and as late as those of anyone in the building.

When you become a head coach, all of a sudden you convince yourself you can now find the time to do both. You do so at great risk. The head coach is held responsible for the outcome of sixteen games. When he takes on the coordinator duties, too, he's judged on the twelve-hundred-plus calls he makes during the year.

I find it interesting that you seldom see a head coach in the NFL who feels compelled to keep his defensive coordinator duties. Wade Phillips was the lone exception in 2008, and he was forced back into it after the Cowboys' lack of defensive productivity threatened their 2008 season. Lovie Smith took on the additional role before the 2009 season. When asked why that was, one longtime defensive coordinator turned head coach explained, "That's because the offensive guys all think they are smarter than us. They are the only ones who can call it."

The main problem I see, besides the time constraints, is that most of the critical decisions you make as a head coach on game day come when you have the ball. If it is fourth and one on your opponent's forty-yard line, outside field goal range, as an offensive play caller you are ready, willing, and able to go for it. It may take the more prudent, larger view of the head coach to provide the sane voice of reason that says, "No, we need to punt this ball."

The difficulty is not only one of time but one of process. When you wake up at 3:00 A.M., what occupies your mind? Is it your cap situation? Is it a question of which eight players are going to be on the inactive list this week? Is it the news conference you have to conduct the next day? Or an off-field incident involving one of your players? Or is it *Should we chip the tackle with the running back on the way out to the flat?* What you are thinking about at 3:00 A.M. is revealing. If you are pondering one question, you are cheating the others. If you are thinking about them all, you are not likely to effectively address any of them.

Jim Fassel had a situation similar to mine in his 2002 season with the Giants, two seasons after we faced each other in the Super Bowl. The Giants had proven to be ineffective in their first six games, going 3–3. Jim took the play calling over from Sean Payton, and the Giants went on a run to a 10–6 record and a first-round loss in the playoffs. The following year Fassel felt he had to hold on to the play-calling duties. The subsequent year, a rash of injuries led to a 4–12 record, and Fassel was fired.

I repeated the same mistake after taking over the play calling in 2006. After six games in that season we were twenty-fifth or worse in just about every measurable offensive category. After going on a 9–1 tear the remainder of the season, we were able to finish in the top ten of virtually every offensive category for the last ten games of the season. We lost in the

Divisional Round to the eventual Super Bowl champion Indianapolis Colts. The next year, I, too, felt compelled to hold on to the play-calling duties. Then our veteran quarterback, Steve McNair, was injured in the first quarter of the season opener. (McNair was hampered by injuries throughout the year and retired after the season. As every NFL fan sadly knows, he was murdered in July 2009.) But in that 2007 season it wasn't just the quarterback; the whole team was riddled with injuries. I was less effective as head coach and as an offensive coordinator because I was trying to do both jobs, and at the end of a 5–11 season, I, too, was fired.

The morning I got fired, I'd driven to work already preoccupied with the burning questions of the new season. I was ready to go down and interview a new offensive coordinator, and my first stop was to be Miami, where Cam Cameron had been fired by the Dolphins. (Weeks later, my successor, John Harbaugh, smartly hired Cam for the offensive coordinator's job.)

Then I walked into Ozzie's office and he gave me the news. Owner Steve Bisciotti came in a few hours later, cordial but firm, and emphasized that while he appreciated my hard work, and understood the mitigating circumstances, and realized that he'd given me assurances that I'd be brought back, the winds had changed and his decision was final.

After Bisciotti left that day, I sat in Ozzie's office. At one point, I said, "Ozzie, I feel stupid here. What did I miss?"

"You didn't miss anything," he said. And then he looked at me for a moment, and said, "You look relieved."

I suppose that for a while I was. I realized that I shouldn't take it personally. I realized that it was only business. I sat in my home that night, and our vice president of communications,

Kevin Byrne, and his wife, Sally, stopped by. We talked, we had a few drinks, and we absorbed the shock.

The hangover from the firing lasted a while. It hurt leaving on someone else's terms. It hurt not being able to say good-bye to men I'd worked with almost daily for years. Until you experience being fired you can't really understand how quickly it changes everything.

Of course, I realized fairly quickly that losing my job wasn't the end of the world, and that everything was going to be okay. Suddenly, the entire cumulative weight of nine seasons—balancing the offense and the defense, keeping Ray Lewis feeling appreciated but also in check, searching for a starting quarterback, suffering through the offensive coordinator's job, dealing with the jibes in the local media—had lifted. For years, I had been paid good money to worry about those things. Now, for the time being, I was going to get paid the same amount of money *not* to worry about those things.

Within a few days I realized that, at some level, I *was* relieved. Coaching the Baltimore Ravens was now someone else's problem.

Of course, I'm a football coach. So within a week, I started missing it. Still do.

"THERE ARE NO CERTAINTIES"

As I entered the grand ballroom of New York's Radio City Music Hall for the 2008 NFL draft I felt as if I were walking into Herod's Temple. The place reeked of money.

Like most coaches, I had never been to the NFL draft. By the time I came into the league in 1992, the day had long since passed when teams actually convened to conduct the "annual selection meeting" in person. In today's NFL the team's owner, coaches, and personnel people are all huddled in their respective war rooms in their local facility, while sending a ceremonial team representative to New York to sit by the phone hour after hour, awaiting directions on which name to put on a card to turn in for a selection.

Like most people, I based my view of the staging of the draft on what I had seen on TV. To actually be there gave me a totally different perspective. The half dozen or so players—the future multimillionaires who are invited to New York for their inevitable first-round selections—are in the eye of the media storm. Among the players, agents, league personnel, marketers, ad agency people, lawyers, posses, and fans, it was more spectacle than working environment.

And believe this: However big you *think* your family is, it will grow in the weeks leading up to your appearance at the NFL draft. At the 2003 draft, Charles Rogers had ninety-eight people in his entourage.

Standing in the midst of it all, I had the same recurring thought: *This is so not about football.* I saw Howie Long, the Raiders' Hall of Famer who was there to watch his son Chris get drafted. We were able to say a quick hello, and it occurred to me that Howie looked as dazed and overwhelmed by the circus as I was.

The fact is the draft, with today's technology and communications capability, could probably be accomplished in about two or three hours, tops (as anyone who's ever engaged in a fantasy football draft can attest, the people who have done their homework already *know* who they want to take when it's their turn to pick). But why do that when you can televise the spectacle, turn it into a two-day viewing bonanza, and draw TV ratings that far exceed the actual NBA and NHL games that compete with it?

A year later, in 2009, when I returned to the draft as a contributor for the NFL Network, the festival had grown even bigger. ESPN began its broadcast five hours *before* the draft began. The league invited nine likely first-rounders to sit in the green room, rather than the four or five of past years. (In so doing, it ensured a replay of recent years, when we'd watch some highly regarded first-rounder sitting restlessly in the green room as his name falls down the draft board and millions fall off his first contract. In 2009, it was Michael Oher, the behemoth Mississippi offensive lineman whose story was memorably captured by Michael Lewis in his book *Blindside*. The Ravens were happy to take him when he fell to the twenty-third pick.)

As this was the very same month that Oprah, your mother,

and half the people in the country were discovering Twitter, Commissioner Roger Goodell tweeted from backstage at the draft ("i told crabtree that at least he gets to keep his same college colors"). Around the league, teams hosted their own draft parties, with tailgating outside the stadium and people paying to gather at team facilities to watch the broadcast.

And why not? The draft has the minute-by-minute suspense of *24* and the *Who Wants to Be a Millionaire?* story line of instant riches. And it speaks to the competitive balance that keeps hope brimming throughout the league. Even Lions fans, coming off the beatdown of an 0–16 season, could look at Matthew Stafford up there with the commissioner, holding up the team's redesigned home jersey, and think, *We could be decent next year.* ESPN's ratings were up by 11 percent in 2009, drawing more viewers on a Saturday afternoon than the Red Sox and Yankees on ESPN's *Sunday Night Baseball* the following night. Overall, the NFL estimated that 39 million people watched some part of the draft.

Of course it's not just the weekend itself. By mid-February, with the scouting combine in Indianapolis, the football draft season is upon us. (What with all the draft preparation, the beginning of the veteran free-agency period, the annual meetings, and the rolling out of the new season's schedule, football is in the news daily from mid-February to the end of April.)

Jake Long, the first pick in the 2008 draft, had agreed before being the number-one overall choice to a five-year $57.75 million contract with the Miami Dolphins. Chris Long of Virginia was the second overall pick, going to the St. Louis Rams for a reported $55 million with a $21 million signing bonus. As Howie Long looked on, he had to be amazed. His son had just signed a contract for more money than Howie made in his entire career, and his son had not played a down in the NFL yet. On the next pick, the Atlanta Falcons landed Matt Ryan, their future star quarterback, to a six-year, $75 million contract with a guarantee of $34 million up front. Superagent Tom Condon was smiling broadly because he represented two of these first three picks in this year's draft.

Within a few days, the players would be flown to the cities where they'd start their professional careers, and after contracts were signed, pose for a photo with the team's owner. The owners' smiles often look more like grimaces, however, and you can understand why. If you've got one of the top few picks, you are looking at signing a player to a contract worth 5 percent to 10 percent of the value of your entire franchise. In an economic recession. Think the owners don't want to be damn sure you've got this one right? Stafford, the top pick in the 2009 draft, signed a deal that pays more guaranteed money—$41.7 million—than any active player in the NFL. That's pressure. And the response of the fans who are eager for their team to get better only heightens the stakes. So coaches and personnel people work nearly around the clock in the spring to make sure they give themselves the best possible chance at success. And then they hope for the best.

As H. L. Mencken once wrote, "The public wants certainties. But there are no certainties."

Mencken would have made a good football scout.

It's been sixty years since the Los Angeles Rams hired a man named Eddie Kotal to be the first traveling scout in professional football. Since then, the area of personnel evaluation has changed dramatically. It's not uncommon for a team to have fifteen to twenty full-time employees in its football personnel department. Scouting players isn't just a division; it's become an industry.

The teams that have had the most success in drafting over the past few years—the Colts, Patriots, Chargers, Titans, Ravens—seem to have done a good job drawing from the two main scouting trees that emerged from the maturation of the scouting process in the seventies and eighties.

The Cowboys, with the development of their computerized scouting system of the sixties, relied on "measurables" (height, weight, speed, arm strength, shuttle speed, and so forth). The 49ers rose up against Dallas at the end of the seventies by being more interested in the intangible elements that couldn't be fed into a computer. (Ironically, it was when the Cowboys went against their measurable recommendations that they really paid the price. When the Cowboys selection came up in the third round of the 1979 draft, the top player available on their board was a quarterback. Tom Landry, feeling the team was deep enough at the position, made the rare decision to go "off the board" and take a tight end, Doug Cosbie, who went on to have a productive career with the team. Six selections after Dallas, the 49ers took the player that the Cowboys had passed on, the Notre Dame quarterback by the name of Joe Montana.)

There's much to recommend both philosophies. The best teams now feel that measurables are important (you don't want a slow, small football team), but so is personality and a player's psychological disposition. "I am convinced that personality and makeup are absolutely critical in predicting a college player's future success, or lack thereof," says one longtime scout. "I don't believe the teams that draft poorly spend enough time or have enough skilled evaluators to really figure out the 'fabric' of the players. The Bengals, Lions, Raiders, and Redskins all come to mind. It's one thing to draft a big and fast receiver like Devin Thomas. It's another thing if he can't learn, stay healthy, or stop running the streets at night."

Many of the most successful teams have their roots in the Cleveland Browns' staff of the early nineties. Those teams were coached by Bill Belichick, with a personnel staff that included Dom Anile, Ozzie Newsome, Phil Savage, Scott Pioli, and George Kokinis.

Belichick, of course, went to New England, and brought along Pioli, who'd started out as a gofer but showed a gift for divining talent. Belichick and Pioli, now the general manager in Kansas City, built a dynasty by focusing less on measurables and more on performance. The team's mantra, composed by Pioli and printed in red at the bottom of each page of the team's scouting handbook, was: "We are building a big, strong, fast, smart, tough, and disciplined football team that consistently competes for championships." Less concerned with "measurables" and forty times than with "game" speed and tangible evidence that players excelled on the field, Pioli recognized the corollary to the interdependence of a football team. It was not the best fifty-three players you could get, it was the best *team* of fifty-three individuals.

The Patriots understood before most teams that in the transient modern age, it was more important than ever that the parts fit, and that the players drafted or signed through free agency be a *particularly* good fit for the style of offense or defense a team favored. For his part, Belichick seemed more concerned with character than he'd been in Cleveland. (Although there are always exceptions. Randy Moss loafed through two seasons at Oakland, but when he came to New England in 2007, he had the greatest season ever by a wide receiver. Belichick deserves credit for taking the chance on a marquee player, then creating an environment in which the player would flourish. Of course, having a quarterback that Moss respected made a world of difference as well.) The quintessential Patriot free-agent signing was Mike Vrabel, who was let go by the Steelers after the 2000 season and went on to be a key cog in the Patriots dynasty of the 2000s. Vrabel didn't have off-the-charts physical skills, but he was a tremendously smart player, and he filled his role perfectly. It wasn't a coincidence that, when he began his rebuilding project as the GM of Kansas City, he traded for Vrabel, to add veteran leadership to a young defense.

In Indianapolis in 1998, Bill Polian brought in Dom Anile, a friend from Polian's coaching days (Anile coached C.W. Post in the early seventies, when Polian was on the staff at the Merchant Marine Academy) who had gone on to become one of the most respected personnel men in football during his days in Cleveland.

Together, Polian and Anile constructed a system that owed its roots to the Dallas Cowboys' computer scouting system from the sixties. They also drew from the concept of video profiling, an innovation of Bill Walsh when he was coaching the 49ers, condensing several games of tape on a player to his best and worst fifteen plays, in an attempt to gauge a player's potential, as well as to get a sense of what kind of mistakes he was consistently making. With the advent of digital technologies this practice has expanded to a level never conceived by Walsh. Most teams will put virtually every college game played into their digital databank and sort the players for a career-long play-by-play view as standard operating procedure. This is particularly true in evaluating quarterbacks. The ability to see every throw, back-to-back, is a huge advantage when one is trying to get a sense of the quarterback's overall play. Likewise, every step taken by a player at the Combine is catalogued and organized so that a scout or coach can now look at any player comprehensively with game tape and combine material in one viewable format.

For some, this has made going to the Combine itself redundant. Aside from the player interviews, some of which are also catalogued and saved, and other face-to-face encounters with an athlete, using the current technology is much more efficient. This, coupled with the live broadcast of the Combine on the NFL Network, makes being at the Combine almost too limiting. A few years back, while I was watching a group work out, Mike Nolan, my former defensive coordinator and then head coach of the San Francisco 49ers, had come up to sit with me to talk. As Mike and I were visiting, my daughter Aubree called me on my cell and chastised me, "Quit talking to Mike and watch the players." Turns out she was watching the NFL Network's coverage of the day, and their cameras had a shot into the stands that showed Mike and me chatting. Way too much documentation going on.

Another old school versus new age contrast at the Combine is the timing of the supposedly all-important, yet in fact virtually pointless, forty-yard dash. This is the premier event at the Combine, even though scout after scout and coach after coach will say the forty time has long been overvalued, that it does not adequately measure "football speed." What is amazing is that even though each runner is electronically timed and those times are shared with all the clubs, the scouts and coaches align themselves along the finish line, each manned with his own stopwatch. Each man has his proprietary way of getting the "right time." Yet as you sit and listen to the cacophony of "beeps" of the stopwatches starting and stopping, it's clear this process only leads to a diverse set of times. I have sat in draft rooms with scouts and coaches together looking at the verified electronic times and often a scout or coach will chime in,

"Well, I had him faster than that," as though in this instance the impartial, laser-activated electronic time was not as valid as the one recorded by hand and with the naked eye.

Back to Polian and Anile: What they added in Indianapolis was their own scale, somewhat modified from earlier ones, in which draftable players were ranked from 5.00 to 7.00. Added to this was a greater reliance on psychological testing and more intensive regression analysis to study the correlation between test results and pro performance. They also honed a system of letter-typing, by which players with potential red flags were more easily classified. Minor scrapes with the law would get a small c, while more serious or more persistent violations would receive a large C. In ten drafts with Polian in charge, the Colts have never drafted a player with a large C designation. "It became a good shorthand," says Anile. "You'd learn to stay away from a player, no matter how good he was, if he had the whole alphabet behind his grade." Thus a player who was a pure 6.56 would be drafted by the Colts ahead of a more talented player whose 6.64cxt indicated concerns about character (c), durability (x), and psychological makeup (t).

The new system was largely in place on the day of the 1999 draft, when Polian dealt the team's best and most productive player, Marshall Faulk, to the St. Louis Rams, for a high first-round draft pick, and then passed on Heisman Trophy winner Ricky Williams to instead select lesser-known University of Miami running back Edgerrin James. The criticism surrounding the choice could be heard throughout the state and across the country. At the end of the first day of the draft, as the Colts' staffers were leaving the war room and finally sensing the degree to which their choice was being vilified by the public, Anile found one of the Colts' interns and gave him his keys, saying, "Here, why don't you go out and start my car for me?"

James was the most controversial draft choice Polian ever made, but as with the year before, when he chose Peyton Manning with the Colts' first overall pick, its wisdom was soon proven. It wasn't merely that James was a better fit for the Colts' offensive system, he was a better all-around player than Williams (and given Williams's history of suspensions related to marijuana, a much better off-the-field risk as well). In 1999, Polian's second season at the helm, the Colts improved from 3–13 to 13–3, the biggest one-season swing in league history, and he won the NFL's General Manager of the Year Award for a record fifth time.

You judge not only people, but schools as well. Ozzie Newsome and I both had very specific and fiercely held views of players from specific schools (his was one in the Midwest and mine was on the West Coast). We both knew that our evaluation of a player from one of these schools was tempered by our admitted bias, and the differences in our biases provided a check-and-balance system so that our biases would not affect the overall selection. Indeed, I think a good many scouts and coaches would admit to having a "gut feeling" about a player that is really nothing more than a collective set of experiences they had had with certain personality traits, physical skills, or success or lack of success with athletes from a particular school.

At Baltimore, the Ravens went against the grain and conventional wisdom time and time again, with success. In the 1996 draft, at a time when even my predecessor as head coach, Ted Marchibroda, was urging Ozzie to take Lawrence Phillips, he stuck to the board and selected Jonathan Ogden, who turned into a perennial All-Pro. Later in the same draft, Ray Lewis was viewed by many as too small to be an impact middle linebacker (just as Mike Singletary had been misjudged a generation earlier), but the Ravens saw how tenacious and tough he was and got the future Hall of Famer with the twenty-sixth pick.

Different systems have slightly different emphases, but the eternal verities remain. "Over time, I began to see a direct link between personality—self-motivated, tough, and smart players—and how they performed," says one veteran scout. "These players may not have been the best testers or the biggest and fastest but they were the most reliable and most consistent. The 'pretty girls' often disappointed us because they weren't tough, smart, durable, or trustworthy."

The ability to consistently find players like that is one of the characteristics of the best teams.

"Nothing good happens after midnight," said Denny Green in his very first speech to his players as head coach of the Vikings in 1992. What was true then is gospel now. Player conduct has become an obsession with the NFL, and all other professional sports.

The first admonition in the player "Code of Conduct" policy issued by the league spells this out very clearly: Engaging in violent or criminal activity is unacceptable and constitutes conduct detrimental to the integrity of and public confidence in the National Football League.

The perception is that Commissioner Roger Goodell has made player conduct the defining issue of his young stewardship. "Players have to understand that playing in the NFL is not a right, it is a privilege," he has said. "A privilege that comes with great rewards, but great responsibility as well."

Goodell has certainly made it a point of emphasis. One has to remember the environment at the time Goodell took over in September 2006. In the span of nine months, nine members of the Cincinnati Bengals were arrested. On New Year's Eve of that year, following a season-ending overtime loss to San Francisco,

Denver Broncos cornerback Darrant Williams was killed in a drive-by shooting outside a nightclub at 2:00 A.M.

After Williams's funeral in Fort Worth, Goodell and Gene Upshaw spoke about the changing nature of the risks facing football players and vowed to work together to address the issue.

That led to a remarkable meeting, with Goodell, Upshaw, Denver Broncos owner Pat Bowlen, and about a dozen active players, held in Indianapolis during the Combine in February 2007. Former Players Association president and fifteen-year veteran Troy Vincent described the meeting by saying, "We all had something at stake. What is paramount is that we preserve our game and control its well-being. This goes beyond collective bargaining. One side can't do it on its own. Everybody needs to be held accountable."

Coming out of Indianapolis, the league enacted a two-pronged approach. Players could expect tougher sanctions (like the year-long suspension of Bengals' receiver Chris Henry, who had in various incidents been charged with marijuana possession, aggravated assault with a firearm, and driving under the influence, among other things), but the league would also devote even more resources to educating players about their rights and responsibilities. It wasn't as if this issue had been overlooked in the previous decade; every team in the NFL had at least one dedicated "player development" director whose responsibility it was to serve as a supplementary conduit for players who needed life-training skills, counseling, sensitivity training—in short, all the things that might fall under the heading of an "employee assistance program" at a more typical job. The league's rookie symposium was expanded to require mandatory attendance by all drafted players and was made more in-depth.

Even as this was happening, there was a feeling among many

of the veteran players in the league that all the education in the world wasn't going to reach certain players. "The ones getting in trouble won't hear it because they don't want to know it," said one player. "They are going to do what they do anyway."

Player behavior is a delicate issue for all concerned. It is coaches who are held accountable for creating and maintaining the "chemistry" and "accountability" in a locker room. Most players will approach a coach about a potential problem, rather than bringing it up with a teammate himself.

The player accused of stepping out of line often tells the person bringing up the issue—be it a coach or a teammate—to "stay out of my lane." The implication is that it's nobody's business but his own. So most players are reluctant to criticize teammates for off-the-field activities, feeling that teammates will be indignant about the reproach.

Yet this is not always the case. I've seen instances where a true team leader possesses the character and gravitas to assert himself, and affect a teammate's behavior.

Having a veteran leader like that can be a powerful aid to a coach.

One example of this type of team leadership came from a young female attorney who specialized in sexual harassment and abuse cases. I would bring her in to lecture my teams every couple of years in hopes they would come to understand the "predatory" environment they were in as professional athletes and what their rights were in these incidents. She told a story of an NBA player who was a client and had related this event: "When I was a rookie, and getting used to being on the road so much, my teammates taught me a valuable lesson. I was in a bar in the hotel late one night and started up a conversation with an attractive young lady. One thing led to another and we ended up going to my room. To my surprise there waiting for me were two of my veteran teammates. They sat me down and the young woman, whom they had hired, laid out the hard truth about groupie scam artists: 'We were going to do such-and-such, then the next day I would have threatened a sexual assault charge in an effort to extort money from you.' The veterans said this lesson was on them, and from here on out I was on my own."

Coaches still say it all over the league as teams get off the bus after a game: "Don't do anything in the next two days that will prevent us from keeping our momentum." Inevitably, players nod, get off the bus, and, every once in a while, go do something stupid.

One issue that has moved to the forefront of public discussion, though it has been on the league's radar for some time, is the propensity for players to carry weapons.

In 2008, the Giants were humming along nicely when Tom Coughlin got one of the calls you dread, the after-midnight call that means something has gone terribly wrong. In this case, it was about Plaxico Burress, the team's gifted wide receiver who had shot himself in the leg while partying in a New York nightclub. Burress was carrying a .40-caliber Glock in his waistband and felt it slipping down his leg; as he grabbed at it, he accidentally pulled the trigger and shot himself in the thigh.

In addition to the personal trauma it caused Burress, who was suddenly in serious legal trouble, the incident destroyed the momentum that the Giants had built. They were an easier team to defend (as the Eagles showed twice in the months following the incident), and they squandered a season of promise with an early playoff exit. When players go down in action on the field, teammates understand it. But players are far less tolerant about teammates taking themselves out of the game by off-field misbehavior.

Marshawn Lynch, running back for the Buffalo Bills, was

subsequently arrested just after the season, also for possession of a gun. Players have the right to carry a weapon, as long as it is properly registered and handled. Neither in Lynch's case nor in Burress's case was the weapon properly registered.

The league is obviously concerned about the potential for an incident far more serious than Burress's accidentally shooting himself in the leg.

"The real issue, to me, is when the players feel they're unsafe, they shouldn't be there," Goodell had said. "So get out, don't be there. If you feel the need to have a firearm to be someplace, you're in the wrong place."

I've heard plenty of fans who dismiss any player's carrying weapons as foolish, and certainly many players are foolish about carrying weapons. But you have to understand what a siege mentality exists among modern NFL players. Think of what happened to the Redskins' Sean Taylor, who was gunned down by intruders in his own home.

More recently, the same week Burress ended his season by shooting himself in the leg, another player—Giants' wide receiver Steve Smith—was robbed at gunpoint. Smith wasn't out on his own, wasn't at a club, and he wasn't foolishly leaving himself exposed. Instead he was taking a chauffeured car back to his town house in a gated community. As he got out of his car, someone held a gun to his head and demanded his jewelry, money, and cell phone.

More so than ever before, players are targets.

Beyond that, of course, there's a degree of common sense that players need to exhibit. And not everyone displays it. But this isn't about people being *unaware* of the illegality of an action. As one longtime coach put it, "Hell, they all know it's illegal. But I am not sure the players think they are doing anything *wrong*."

In the case of Michael Vick, and the despicable acts committed involving the dogs he owned and bred, that was certainly the case. Vick may not have understood the degree of public outrage that the dogfighting revelations would create, but he certainly knew that what he was doing was socially unacceptable and illegal. He kept that part of his life carefully hidden from the Falcons, and when the allegations began to surface and he was summoned to New York to meet with Roger Goodell, he apparently lied to the commissioner about the degree of his involvement.

Now, of course, Vick has become the face of the grievous legal consequences for inappropriate off-field behavior. But in all these instances (weapons, marijuana, and dogfighting), the league is contending with social, generational, geographical, and cultural differences that affect players' attitudes about their rights and personal choices.

The discussion of a player's character begins long before he ever comes into the league. While some teams ignore character and then pay a price, others are far too superficial in their scrutiny. There was a time in the nineties when certain teams didn't want any players with dreadlocks. But people with silly biases like that don't stay employed very long in this game. The key is to know when you are taking a risk—and what kind of a risk you're taking.

In 2008, the Oakland Raiders gave a six-year, $60 million contract with a $26 million signing bonus to Darren McFadden, a player some had dropped down their draft boards due to character questions stemming from a number of off-the-field incidents he had been involved in.

McFadden's case shows clearly that the character evaluation

process in the NFL is not a moral or ethical one, but an economic one. When one GM was asked about taking McFadden early in the first round, where he was projected, he proclaimed, "We took him off our first-round board. We question his character and whether we would want him on our team." When pressed further about whether he would consider him in the second round if he was still there, the same GM stepped off his moral soapbox and said, "That would be a different situation. We would not be risking the same thing. He might be worth the risk at that pick."

And that's how it goes.

"We've tweaked this," says one longtime personnel man. "We spent more time than ever before talking about a player's STIC [speed, toughness, intelligence, character]. We're less interested in how a player runs than how he interviews. You've got to play well on tape, you've got to be a good football player. If you are a tough and a good kid, then you are a match."

It's all become much more sophisticated. The interview conditions—usually fifteen minutes in rapid-fire succession during an evening at the Combine—are tightly constructed, and the athletes have been so well trained by their agents it is sometimes hard to get to the essence of a young man (as if that can be done in fifteen minutes anyway). The agents have recognized that in today's world the NFL has knowledge of virtually every move or transgression a player has been involved with since high school. The current procedure adopted by many athletes is to come into the room and immediately outline the circumstance of whatever issue the player was involved in and either explain why they were not responsible, or where applicable, take full responsibility and in doing so impressing the clubs with their supposed maturation and newfound sense of accountability. These declarations become so rote, and the athlete regurgitates his lines in the twenty to twenty-five interviews he does, that it becomes hard to tell whether the soliloquy is real or just really well rehearsed. Ravens' owner Steve Bisciotti, who made his fortune in personnel-related business, came up with a great question to get athletes off their scripts. He suggested, when the athlete was done with his well-rehearsed speech, that we quickly follow up with, "Okay, so what is the worst thing you ever got away with?" You should see some of the confused looks that follow that question. You know that some players are thinking, "Okay, are they aware of something I did not confess to, and if so will they hold it against me for not fessing up to it, or am I now about to admit to something they knew nothing about?" It's a moral dilemma, with millions of dollars at stake.

About ten years ago, I was sitting in a room with one athlete, looking at his file. There was a series of incidents that needed to be addressed, but by then everyone was tired. I didn't want to go down the list event by event and I was pretty sure he didn't either.

I closed the folder and looked him in the eye. "Look," I said, "you're either a thug, or you're stupid. Which is it?"

He eyed me levelly for a moment, then asked, "Are those my only two choices?"

I knew then that he wasn't stupid. As it turned out, he wasn't a thug, either. He played in the NFL for nine successful years, and never had another spot of trouble.

Determining a player's character is not simply a case of "good guys" or "bad guys." Young people sometimes do stupid things. We all have done things in our lives about which our level of embarrassment or accountability depended strictly on whether we were caught. Akin to the philosophical question of whether a tree falling in the forest makes a sound if no one is there to hear it or the question, Is it speeding if you don't get a ticket for it?

One young man, when asked if he had ever been arrested or suspended from his team, answered, "No, sir, never. Well, there was that one time after the frat party, but I was never charged, so no, sir. Well, there was another time outside of a bar when I was, but no, I didn't get charged then either, so no, sir. Well, then there was the one time when I got pulled over, but that got expunged from the record, so no, sir, never." It was like a bad Mike Wallace interview being conducted solo. We did not say a thing, and he just kept going on and on. You want to stop him and say, "You know we can hear you, right?"

When all is said and done, the only real determination you can make is whether a young person just made a mistake or there is a pattern that shows the athlete has a character flaw that may come back to haunt him (and the team drafting him). This reminds me of the Bill Cosby routine in which someone tries to explain to Cosby that his use of cocaine is simply a way of "expanding on who I am. Making me more of what I am." To which Cosby replied, "Yeah, but you are a jerk." If a player is a jerk to start with, it's quite likely that giving him $20 million will only make him a bigger jerk.

With a salary cap in place, teams also have to get ahead. Think about it: You're gambling on expensive, highly drafted rookies and on overpaying free agents. Even when you keep your own players, you are often paying at least market value. The only reliable place you can get bargains is in the draft.

The teams that get ahead do so by finding some way to get value for less than other teams pay for it. They find bargains at positions where other teams pay full price: The Colts don't spend big money on outside linebackers. The Denver Broncos have been one of the best running teams in football for more than a decade, but they rarely spend a top draft choice on a running back.

With New England, the Patriots' finding Tom Brady in the sixth round didn't merely mean a few years of savings before awarding him a fat contract commensurate with his accomplishments. They didn't have to spend a high first-round draft pick on a quarterback and could use those prime selections to stock other positions.

Take a look at two teams that have been consistently strong playing a 3-4—the Patriots and Steelers—and you'll notice that neither of them has built the defense around premium, high-round linebackers. The Patriots won three Super Bowls and went to another this decade thriving almost exclusively on imported linebackers: Mike Vrabel, Roosevelt Colvin, Adalius Thomas, Junior Seau. Rather than risk a high draft pick on someone who might or might not pan out, Bill Belichick often lets other people train them, then he brings them over.

Pittsburgh, even after Bill Cowher's exit, has drafted athletic, often-unheralded linebackers on the second day of the draft (or in the case of 2008 defensive player of the year James Harrison, signed them as undrafted free agents), then plugged them into the Steelers' system. The players come and go—Pittsburgh famously lets many of its big-money free agents walk—but the system continues to thrive.

In 2008, on the way to their second Super Bowl win in four seasons, the Steelers ranked first in the NFL in defensive total yards allowed and rushing yards allowed, and fourth and fifth, respectively, in points allowed and passing yards allowed. What is even more impressive is who they did it with. Defensive coordinator Dick LeBeau's defense does not require a stable of All-Pros. In 2008, according to *USA Today*'s salary survey, the

Steelers had a total of $128.8 million in salaries, of which the defense is responsible for only 37 percent at $48 million (the salary cap in 2008 was $116.7 million, but the Steelers' figure includes bonuses paid out in 2008 and prorated over future years of contracts). Compare that to the Ravens' $90.7 million in total salaries, of which the defense accounted for 65 percent, at $59 million. Only four of the top ten Steelers salaries are on the defensive side of the ball, while eight of the top ten highest-paid Ravens are on the defense.

A clear philosophy and preparation help, but when it comes down to it, you still need to be able to respond calmly to all the surprises of draft weekend. Teams that fall in love with one player, then panic when they don't get him, or don't account for the possibility that they'll have an offer to move up or down in the draft, rarely wind up ahead of the game.

Bill Walsh in the eighties and Jimmy Johnson and Jerry Jones in the nineties built dynasties partly by understanding that they could help themselves with quantity if they understood not only what sort of players they needed, but how the rest of the league valued those players.

One of the wildest draft days I remember came in 2003. The Ravens knew they needed a quarterback—we'd gone as far as we could with retreads and castoffs, even winning a Super Bowl, but we needed to build the team around a reliable starter for the future—but also had other pressing needs. In particular, we were interested in Carson Palmer, Byron Leftwich, and Kyle Boller.

After debating for a while, Marvin Lewis, my old defensive coordinator for our Super Bowl team, who had become head coach of the Cincinnati Bengals, made Carson Palmer the first pick of the 2003 draft. As the picks clicked off, Ozzie New-some made a run at moving up from the tenth pick and get-ting Leftwich, who was higher on our board than Boller. Ozzie knew that James "Shack" Harris, the GM for the Jacksonville Jaguars and our former director of pro personnel, was going to take Leftwich with the eighth pick of the draft, two spots in front of us. Ozzie started working the phones with Minnesota, which had the seventh overall pick and wanted to move down in the order. It looked as if we had a deal, until Jacksonville, knowing we were trying to move up, engaged Minnesota with the same talks, offering to move up one pick to ensure they got Leftwich. As the clock ticked down, Minnesota got greedy and kept playing one side against the other.

Ozzie had a hard-and-fast rule that no trade could get done in time with less than two minutes on the clock, and we were approaching the deadline quickly. Mike Tice, my former line coach when I was with the Vikings, and now their head coach, was working the deal. I finally pulled the phone from Ozzie and said, "Mike, you have to pull the trigger on this one way or the other because we are running out of time. Decide!"

Once Ozzie got the phone back he was able to get the deal done, but knew we were probably out of time. It is the proto-col of the draft that the team getting the pick is responsible for phoning in the deal. As we quickly dialed the league number, it was busy—as were the secondary numbers we had. Ozzie knew this was not going to get done. To this day I believe that Shack masterfully stretched the conversation out with Min-nesota so as to get his player and not have to give anything up in the process.

Quickly, Ozzie told our man at the draft to write two names on two different cards: Byron Leftwich and Terrell Suggs. Through all this we were amazed that Suggs had fallen down the board. During our ramp-up to the draft, when we "read our players" to rank on the board, Ozzie said, "We will do Suggs, but it is a waste of time. He is never going to get past the fourth or fifth pick."

The board already showed some surprises: After Palmer, the next two players taken were wide receivers, Charles Rogers by the Lions and Andre Johnson by the Texans. After DeWayne Robertson went to the Jets and Terence Newman to the Cowboys, the Saints drafted next (right before Minnesota) and chose Johnathan Sullivan, a defensive tackle from Georgia who would be a bust and out of the league in three years. The Saints would rue that selection for years, as four of the next five players taken would be Pro Bowlers.

If your time allotment during the draft lapses, the next team has the right to turn in its pick until the original team drafting in that spot does so. The time elapsed on Minnesota, and Jacksonville turned in their card on Leftwich. Watching this transpire, the next team, at the ninth pick, was Carolina, and fearful that Minnesota could jump back in at any time, they had their pick of Jordon Gross ready to go. Gross was the highest-rated offensive tackle on the board and the Panthers had made no secret that they coveted him. Now we were on the clock, but again, Minnesota could jump in at any time. Ozzie was yelling on the phone to turn in the card, fearful that Minnesota had regrouped and would pick Suggs. Minnesota had made a decision, but instead chose Kevin Williams, who became an All-Pro defensive tackle. We wound up with Suggs, a player we thought was worthy of being the third or fourth pick of the draft and who would become one of the premier pass rushers in the league.

Normally, the room would have erupted at our good fortune, but we immediately went to work on trying to trade back up into the first round to get the final quarterback remaining, Kyle Boller. Phil Savage had done his homework and was prepared, in the event a player like Suggs had fallen down the board and would prevent us from taking Boller, the tenth-rated player on our board. (We would later get him, and more about that in the next chapter.)

We'd scouted Suggs plenty and liked what we saw. He had one of the most explosive and powerful first steps—"get-offs," in scout speak—we had ever seen, and Rex Ryan was all but drooling over the chance to get him.

There were skeptics, because in a couple of workouts leading up to the draft, Suggs had not run well, particularly in the forty-yard dash. One of the first questions I fielded after the selection was announced was a query about his slow forty-yard-dash time. "Well," I said, "if the quarterback takes a forty-yard drop, we may be in trouble."

We got Suggs that draft because we and other teams have learned what to value and what to disregard. In general, teams know what sort of running backs excel in pro football. They've gotten very good at developing a profile of the sort of talent it takes to be a successful offensive tackle (the top two selected in the 2008 draft, Boise State's Ryan Clady to Denver and Virginia's Branden Albert to Kansas City, started every game of their rookie seasons). As a group, we are smarter and more sophisticated about nearly every position on the field—with the notable exception of the most important position, quarterback. When it comes to evaluating quarterbacks, we take off the scientist's lab coat. When it comes to quarterbacks, collectively we're still like a bunch of blindfolded kids at a birthday party, swinging wildly in hopes that we'll break open the piñata.

"NOBODY KNOWS ANYTHING"

The Academy Award–winning screenwriter William Goldman (*Butch Cassidy and the Sundance Kid, Marathon Man*) says there is a key rule that you must always remember to understand the way things work in Hollywood: "Nobody knows anything."

When it comes to pro football, the same phrase applies to the complex, tortured exercise of deciding who can and who can't play quarterback . . . there's something of an art to it, but all attempts at science have failed.

Back in the late 1960s, teams succeeded only about 50 percent of the time in identifying quarterbacks taken in the first ten selections of the draft, where you'd want everyone you pick to be a future All-Pro. Overall, in the entire first round, where you at least want a longtime quality starter, their collective record was identical, about 50 percent. Sometimes they were right (as when the Pittsburgh Steelers took Terry Bradshaw with the first pick in the 1969 draft) and sometimes they were flat wrong (as when the Chargers took Marty Domres with the ninth pick in the 1968 draft). Sometimes they made selections that, in retrospect, seem implausible. In 1967, with the third pick in the draft, the San Francisco 49ers chose Heisman Trophy winner Steve Spurrier, the future "ball coach," from Florida. One pick later, the Miami Dolphins took future Hall of Famer Bob Griese.

Today, with the benefit of decades more experience, a keener understanding of the qualities needed to be successful, and millions more spent in scouting and evaluating talent with precision . . . teams still are hitting about 50 percent when trying to identify future All-Pro quarterbacks in the first ten picks, and the same 50 percent with first-rounders in general.

There are two ineluctable truths that one can never forget about the position of quarterback: (1) It is the single most difficult position to master in the world of team sports. No other position—not baseball pitcher or soccer goalkeeper or basketball point guard—requires such a mixture of athletic skills, raw brainpower, functional intelligence, and that ineffable something that Hemingway once described as "grace under pressure." (2) It is the single hardest position to evaluate in all of professional sports. NFL teams, armed with three or four years of major college game films, hundreds of pages of scouting reports, dozens of hours of workouts in Indianapolis, private team workouts, and personal interviews, will still miss routinely.

The franchise quarterback is the Holy Grail of the football business. The search for one gives people careers and ends careers. Draft the right quarterback and everything else you do instantly looks smarter. Pick the wrong one and you can start working on your résumé. The quest to land one—and the fear of missing one—gets into the heads of football people. It has humbled much smarter people than me. Sooner or later, it can cause everyone in the game to veer from their principles, abandon strategy, and . . . reach.

Consider this: From 1999 to 2008, there were twenty-eight quarterbacks drafted in the first round of the draft, but only eleven drafted in the second round. Think about that: By all rights, the distribution from one round to the next should be roughly equal. Even if teams tend to overrate or overvalue quarterbacks, they should overrate them and overvalue them all the way down the line. But that's not what happens. Teams worry nearly as much about *passing* on a franchise quarterback as they do about drafting a player who turns out to be a bust.

In other positions, there is a rough pecking order based on the skill set that a prospect shows: This wide receiver has both the speed and the hands to be a first-round draft choice, while this receiver isn't fast enough to justify a first-round pick. But with quarterbacks, too many of the elements are intangible to begin with, or impossible to reliably project from one level to the next, so players with the size and the arm strength tend to go in the first round, even if there are good reasons—makeup, composure, leadership skills—to suspect they won't succeed at this level.

Remember Cade McNown? The quarterback from UCLA was the twelfth player taken in the 1999 draft. He had a decent arm and had enjoyed some college success. But you had to wonder about him. He pleaded guilty to a misdemeanor charge of illegally using a handicapped parking placard while he was at college. Lord knows that other players at other positions have committed far worse offenses during their college days. But you can have a cornerback or an offensive lineman with a bad attitude and a sense of entitlement and it might actually make him a better player. It's different with quarterbacks. McNown's minor violation, that small red flag, always stuck with me. That's not the person I want leading my team. (As it turned out, those who had doubts were right. McNown lacked the pocket presence necessary for the position, and didn't endear himself to his teammates on the Bears. He was out of pro football within three years.)

Quarterback is the most pressurized, most important position on the field. And because the pay is the highest—and rookies cost so much—you really can't afford to miss in the top half of the first round. If you do you can set your franchise back five or ten years.

Take a look at some of the most publicized misses of recent years: Tim Couch and Alex Smith, drafted first overall by Cleveland and San Francisco in 1999 and 2005, respectively; Ryan Leaf, picked second overall by San Diego in 1998; Joey Harrington (Detroit), Heath Shuler (Washington), and Akili Smith (Cincinnati), picked third in 1998, 1999, and 2002. What do all these players have in common? The coaches who were there when these players were drafted are all out of jobs now. From 1992 through 2001 eighteen quarterbacks were selected in the first round. Six went on to have successful NFL careers while twelve were unquestioned busts. Not one of the coaches of the twelve busts had his job three years later. If you're a GM or a head coach and you miss with a top pick at quarterback, you can go ahead and put your house on the market, because you'll be moving soon.

When it goes right—when you pick right, as the Steelers did in 1969 or the Colts did in 1998—you have at least a decade during which you feel that you have a significant practical and psychological edge on almost every team you face. That's a nice thing to take into work week in and week out.

The classic, quintessential case of getting it right occurred in the 1998 draft. The Indianapolis Colts had just hired Bill Polian to take over their football operations, and the Colts had the first pick in the draft. Polian was faced with choosing between two blue-chip quarterbacks, and though his ultimate decision may seem obvious in retrospect, it was anything but at the time. On one hand, there was the Tennessee All-American Peyton Manning, a coach on the field and well-known beast in the film room, whose stock fell slightly as a senior simply because his team didn't win the national title, and he didn't win the Heisman Trophy. Then there was Washington State's burly Ryan Leaf, who at six-foot-five and 245 pounds had the prototypical physique for a pro pocket passer, and was thought by many scouts to be less polished but with a significantly higher upside. (Manning still bristles, ten years later, at how he felt when he was told at age twenty-two that he didn't have much of an "upside" left.)

Had they gone solely on game scouting from the previous fall, the Colts likely would have selected Leaf. But in the months leading up to the draft, Polian bunkered down in his new office and spent most of his time, roughly five hundred hours, watching film and analyzing the comparative strengths of the two quarterbacks. He and his staff watched each of Manning's 1,505 college passes, and each of Leaf's 880 throws, viewing the passes from the 1997 season twice over again. From that epic act of overanalysis came a deeper level of understanding.

"From a pure scouting standpoint, you would have taken Leaf in a heartbeat," says Polian. "Now, as it turns out, when you really got into analysis, even the physical, there were perceptions about Manning that were untrue. There were perceptions about Leaf that were untrue, but your eye sees what it sees and your ear hears what it hears, so scouts came back and said, 'Manning has a weak arm.' When you analyzed every pass they threw for the years that they were in school, that wasn't true. But no scout has the ability to do that. You can only do that in the off-season when you can put together all the film. I remember remarking to Tom Moore [the Colts' longtime offensive coordinator] how astounded I was by the fact that Peyton threw a heavier ball with many more revolutions per second than Leaf. Even [in] the physical part of it, the initial reports were wrong and the conventional wisdom and hype was 100 percent wrong."

And, of course, Polian's selection was 100 percent right. Manning started from his first game, and though the Colts went 3–13 his rookie year, it was clear that Indianapolis had its franchise quarterback.

The true difference between the two quarterbacks proved to be the emotional maturity and work ethic of Manning versus Leaf. Like everyone else, I was enamored of the physical skills of Leaf and had bought in to the "lack of upside" in Manning. I was with the Vikings at the time and we were not picking until the twenty-first pick (Randy Moss), so obviously the evaluation of these two quarterbacks was an academic exercise in that both were going to be long gone by the time we were selecting. Still, we did our homework on players like this because in the age of free agency you never knew when they might become available at a later date.

On the way to the Combine I happened to be on a flight next to Ryan Leaf, also on his way to work out at the Combine. He looked a lot bigger to me than I had expected from watching his game film, so I asked him how much he thought he weighed. He said he had not been working out as regularly as during the season, but he guessed he was in the 235–240 range.

The next day as I sat in the back of the room watching the quarterbacks being weighed and measured, Leaf—seeing a familiar face—gave me a smile as he jumped on the scales. "Two hundred sixty-nine pounds," the scout in charge of weighing the players yelled out. Leaf shot me a look of total surprise when he heard that number.

The next time I visited with Leaf was before the Vikings' game with the San Diego Chargers in the last preseason game of the 1998 season. He had looked good in the preseason and the expectations were sky-high. I asked him how he was doing and he said, "I don't know what all the fuss is about NFL defenses. I have seen about everything they can throw at me and it's no big deal."

You like confidence, but . . .

Three short years and thirty-six interceptions compared to just sixteen touchdown passes later, the young Mr. Leaf realized that he didn't know what he didn't know, and that it *was* a big deal.

Today the Chargers are still catching grief for drafting Leaf, which is a little bit unfair. Even if you had Manning slotted above Leaf on your board (and not everyone did), almost everyone else in pro football projected him as a top-five pick.

Nobody knows anything.

Bill Devaney, the GM for the St. Louis Rams, was part of the scouting group for the Chargers and remembers the red flags they had on Leaf. "We did all the psychological profiles," Devaney says. "There was a guy that we hired at the Redskins—and they're still using this guy at the Combine, Harry Wachs [an optometrist who specialized in a field called visual-cognitive evaluation]. It's a visual thing. His batting average is pretty good. We asked the Redskins if we could use him just for Ryan, and they said yes. It turned out the testing hit him to the letter. Still, we thought we could work through all that. Sometimes you can get in your own way trying to justify or refute all the different data you get."

It's not just rookie quarterbacks who are hard to evaluate. The first regular-season game I coached as a head coach was in St. Louis in 1999, with the Ravens visiting the St. Louis Rams.

On the field, before the game, I shook hands with Dick Vermeil, who wished me luck. Dick was still grieving over the season-ending injury of the Rams' starting quarterback, Trent Green, two weeks earlier in the preseason, that shut down his potentially explosive offense. He allowed that they were going to try to get the team's backup, an Arena League alum named Kurt Warner, to hold the pieces together until they could teach new backup Paul Justin the offense.

Vermeil didn't know what he had—and that's not meant as a criticism. Neither did anyone else. Warner went on to be the league's MVP that season, leading the Rams to a Super Bowl win and launching a career that, after he led the Cardinals to Super Bowl XLIII, might still land him in Canton. It's not only the move from playing in college to pro. You often can't tell about what sort of player a quarterback is going to be until he starts—and, of course, in a culture in which up to a third of the league's head coaches can get fired in any given year, you can't really afford to experiment at great length. And yet think of the Pro Bowl quarterbacks in recent years who started out as backups or retreads—Warner, Tony Romo, Derek Anderson, Matt Hasselbeck, Trent Green, Rich Gannon. The list goes on.

When Tom Brady went down in the 2008 season opener, there was plenty of clucking around the league, and I heard from more than a few people that Bill Belichick was going to pay for not having a reliable backup quarterback. You know the rest: Matt Cassel led New England to an 11–5 season and proved to be such a valuable commodity that the Patriots placed the franchise tag on him, meaning Cassel, who before 2008 hadn't started a football game since high school, was slated to make $14 million in 2009. With Brady's recovery looking good, the Patriots dealt Cassel to the Kansas City Chiefs for a second-round draft choice. Had Brady not gone down, no one would have known what Cassel was capable of.

Nobody knows anything.

So, you're thinking to yourself: Find an expert. Find someone who knows. Someone with a track record.

Over the past twenty years, no one has had a better track record than former Packers GM Ron Wolf: In his days building the Tampa Bay Buccaneers from the ground up, he pulled the trigger on Doug Williams. At Green Bay, he traded for Brett Favre, but also drafted Mark Brunell, Matt Hasselbeck, and Aaron Brooks. All of them developed, all of them not just met but exceeded expectations.

He has an eye. If anyone knows quarterbacks it's Ron Wolf.

And yes, he would have taken Manning over Leaf. But he also points out that virtually everyone who preferred Manning still would have taken Leaf second overall. And Wolf has no pretensions to being the Quarterback Soothsayer.

"Never mind Manning versus Leaf," he says. "I thought Heath Shuler was going to be a Pro Bowler."

One of the main reasons I'm calling games for Fox and not still coaching games for the Baltimore Ravens is that I was unable to develop a Pro Bowl quarterback during my nine years in Baltimore. It wasn't for lack of trying.

As I mentioned earlier, we knew going into the 2003 NFL draft that we had to get a quarterback. With the nineteenth pick in the 2003 draft, we selected Kyle Boller of California. He'd excelled in a pro-style offense and had a live arm and a good head on his shoulders.

Phil Savage, then our director of personnel, had been tracking Boller all year and got more and more excited about him as the year went on. The three main names coming out of that draft at quarterback were Carson Palmer from USC, Byron Leftwich from Marshall, and Boller. Each had all the credentials, and all were projected as early first-round picks.

At the Combine we just happened to have all three of these quarterback interviews back to back to back. Even though each interview lasted only fifteen minutes, you got a clear picture of the differences in the quarterbacks' personalities by speaking with them consecutively. Each man had excellent measurables, but as is usually the case, each had one little qualifier. Scouts and coaches alike always end up with a qualifier about even the best of players, so that if a player doesn't turn out as projected, they can say, "Well, I did say he had . . ."

For these three, the qualifiers were very specific. With Palmer, people were worried about his leadership ability. He did not seem to have a lot of the charisma that you normally associate with a quarterback. Although he is a bright and intelligent young man, you came out of the interview not real fired up about him as a leader. Such was not the case with the next two. Leftwich and Boller had tremendous energy and leadership ability. The concerns with Leftwich were his previous injuries and his lack of mobility in the pocket. For Boller it was his accuracy.

Like Bill Devaney and the Charger group with Leaf, we convinced ourselves in each case that the minuses were not justified. With Palmer, we liked enough of the rest that we thought he could grow into the leadership role. With Leftwich we convinced ourselves that his mobility was no worse than that of a lot of NFL quarterbacks. With Boller, we decided that the lack of quality receivers at Cal was a significant part of the reason for his lack of accuracy.

Eventually, we were able to secure the New England Patriots' first-round pick, the nineteenth overall, which we used to take Boller. Within a couple of years, we learned that Boller's inaccuracy was not a result of the poor receivers at Cal but of Kyle's occasional nervousness in the pocket, which led to his faltering at critical times and has left him a sub-60-percent completion guy thus far in his career.

So it didn't work out for Boller or me. I left after the 2008 season. The Ravens *still* needed a quarterback. So Ozzie and the personnel department worked diligently to scout the next round of athletes. They worked out Matt Ryan and Brian Brohm and Chad Henne. They also took a day and worked out Joe Flacco, a strong-armed kid who had started at Pittsburgh and then transferred to Division I-AA power Delaware.

The process was the same, as were the people doing the evaluating, except that now Cam Cameron, the new offensive coordinator and former head coach of the Miami Dolphins, was involved. Cam had been fired from Miami after the 2007 season and was heavily criticized for taking quarterback John Beck from my alma mater, BYU, with the fortieth pick in the 2007 draft. (The Dolphins released him in April 2009.) The 50/50 rule remained in full effect. The Ravens went 50/50 on the picks of Boller, then Flacco, while Cameron, as an individual, went 50/50 on the picks of Beck and Flacco. Flacco was not asked to win games, only to manage them. With a cannon arm, good pocket presence, and a calm, unruffled demeanor, he quarterbacked the Ravens into the 2008 AFC Championship Game.

Conclusion: There is much that can be learned from the increased precision in scouting (certainly, completion percentage is looked at much more closely than it was ten or fifteen years ago) and from the changing nature of the pro game. And you certainly want to do the kind of intense, fine-grained homework the Colts did when deciding between Manning and Leaf.

But in the end, despite all the tools at our disposal, the challenge of projecting quarterbacks largely defies analysis. We don't know anything. It's a crapshoot.

• • •

The task of identifying the quarterbacks of the future isn't getting easier. There's an apples and oranges problem that's getting worse. It's difficult to project quarterbacks in the spread offenses in college into the multiple offenses of the pros. Then there are other unknowable factors, such as how quarterbacks will cope at the next level with the myriad necessary adjustments—quick audibles at the line of scrimmage, complex hot reads and outlets once the ball is snapped, a torrent of defensive schemes all expertly disguised to prevent detection, and voice signals in the helmet receiver rather than hand signals on the sideline.

The spread gun offenses are an effective use of the talent available to the college game, but the attributes that it takes to run this type of system do not often translate into the NFL. Quarterbacks like Sam Bradford at Oklahoma, Tim Tebow at Florida, Vince Young at Texas, and JaMarcus Russell at LSU put up obscene numbers in their college careers. At first blush these numbers would seem to be ready-made for the pro game. Their completion percentages, yards per attempt, and touchdown-to-interception ratios were all stunning. Yet a quarterback from this style of play has yet to make an impact at the NFL level. Vince Young completed 65 percent of his passes in his last year of college, with a 26–10 touchdown-to-interception ratio. JaMarcus Russell was an otherworldly 68 percent, with twenty-eight TDs and only eight interceptions. But both players struggled to attain even 50 percent completion percentages in the NFL.

Mike Leach at Texas Tech, Urban Meyer at Florida, and Steve Spurrier at the University of South Carolina are three of the most successful and innovative coaches in the history of college football. Their ability, particularly in developing quarterbacks, is beyond question. The names of their quarterbacks litter the record books and honor rolls of college football. What they haven't done yet is produce a quarterback from these systems who's been successful as a starter in the NFL. (This is not to fault them: It's their job to produce winning *college* quarterbacks, not winning pro ones.)

The spread gun systems being run in the college game are a brilliant combination of high-percentage passes, strong running games, and to a large degree, the ability of the quarterback to generate yards rushing from the gun position. And that last piece is crucial, because that's more or less impossible to do on a regular basis in the NFL.

Let's look at these factors and the way they translate to the NFL. Completion percentage is now the hot button for evaluation of quarterbacks. The numbers being put out by this style of play are impressive, but deceiving. The circumstances that allow a quarterback to excel in this system rarely exist in the NFL. Typically, the quarterback is dumping the ball off on a short pass after an effective play fake in which the defense has to honor both the running back and the potential of the quarterback to pull the ball out and run. This puts a great deal of pressure on college defenses and makes for more wide-open receivers and tight ends down the field with little pressure on the quarterback while he throws. In direct contrast, the number-one attribute an NFL quarterback has to have is the ability to operate in the pocket while under a huge amount of pressure.

A key component, especially with players like Tebow and Young, is their ability to run the ball. Certainly, the ability to make plays with his legs outside the structure of an offense is an added benefit of the athletic quarterback. Teams have come to covet this type of athlete in the NFL because of the pressure he puts on the defense. But the trouble is that the modern incarnation of this type of quarterback has yet to win consistently in the NFL and has yet to win a championship. The last championship quarterback who was a consistent threat to scramble was Steve Young, on the 49ers teams of the nineties (before Young, you have to go back to Roger Staubach with the Cowboys in the seventies).

What was true then is still true now: You don't want your quarterback taking any more hits than is absolutely necessary. In the word of one longtime GM, if you want to commit to this style of play with quarterbacks who can run, "You had better have two of them because the first one is going to get hurt."

As much as defensive coordinators hate the pressure an athletic quarterback puts on them, they will tell you they fear the guy who can beat you from the pocket more. Steve Young is probably the last quarterback to challenge this theory, but even he admits, "It wasn't until I showed I could beat you from the pocket that I was able to capitalize on my athletic ability above and beyond the design of the offense."

The biggest concern a coach has is the possibility of injury to his starting quarterback. This can happen easily enough just within the normal course of a game, and exposing your franchise player to additional hits in the running game, with designed runs by the quarterback, only increases that chance of injury.

Vince Young may be the most imposing athlete ever to come out of college at the quarterback position. The Tennessee Titans took Young with the third pick of the 2006 NFL draft, behind Mario Williams and Reggie Bush. The Titans knew they would have to commit to the unique style of play that Vince Young represented. You didn't want to ignore the running skills that helped Texas win a national championship. At the same time, his strong arm lacked consistency, and he was someone around whom you'd have to adapt an offensive system.

Young's NFL numbers are telling. His first-year completion percentage was typical of most first-year quarterbacks. The career 61 percent passer in college dropped to a predictable 51 percent in the NFL. The next year, 2007, he was able to increase his percentage to a solid 62 percent, but threw seventeen interceptions to only nine TD passes. In the third year he was injured and went into a funk that had friends and family fearing for his personal well-being. He was replaced by aging veteran Kerry Collins and was unable to regain the starting position after Collins took the Titans on an AFC-best 13–3 run in 2008 and then were knocked out in the divisional round of the playoffs. What is most impressive about the Titans' run is that Collins was the absolute anti-Young at quarterback. They had to totally change their system and style of play with Collins at quarterback compared to what they spent three years developing with Young.

But don't let me make it sound as if the difficulty in projecting college quarterbacks into the pros is a recent phenomenon. Quarterbacks have *always* been hard to project. A look at the Heisman Trophy quarterbacks paints a bleak picture of their prospects in the NFL. In the past twenty-five years, at least seven Heisman winners—Andre Ware, Gino Torretta, Charlie Ward, Danny Wuerffel, Chris Weinke, Eric Crouch, and Jason White—have been certified washouts as pros.

In 1979, Bill Walsh went to Kentucky to work out a strong-armed prospect from Morehead State named Phil Simms. Walsh was just beginning his career with the San Francisco 49ers and was not yet regarded as a revolutionary genius. As Simms progressed through the workout he started throwing the ball harder and harder, trying to impress the coach. After a while Walsh stepped in and instructed Simms to "try throwing it a little easier." After a few more, Walsh insisted he ease up a little more. "He just kept repeating, 'easier, easier,'" said Simms. "At one point I thought about throwing it underhand." Walsh knew Simms had a big arm; what he didn't know was whether he had the ability to take something off the ball and be more accurate.

As it turned out, the 49ers did not have a first-round pick that first year and Simms obviously impressed the rest of the NFL with his abilities enough to be taken by the New York Giants with the seventh overall pick. Walsh had to settle for taking a quarterback in the third round, with the eighty-second overall selection: Joe Montana. (Besides Simms, there were two other quarterbacks drafted in the first round that year: Jack Thompson of Washington State went third to the Cincinnati Bengals and Steve Fuller of Clemson went twenty-third to the Kansas City Chiefs. Only one of the three first-rounders enjoyed a successful career.)

You grow up thinking there will always be great quarterbacks. And you look back through time, and there almost always have been. In 1970, there were seven Hall of Fame quarterbacks starting for NFL teams—Johnny Unitas, Joe Namath, Len Dawson, Sonny Jurgensen, Fran Tarkenton, Bob Griese, Bart Starr, plus Roger Staubach and Terry Bradshaw coming up, and yet another future Hall of Famer, George Blanda, coming off the bench to steal the headlines. In 1990, you could see Joe Montana, John Elway, Troy Aikman, Warren Moon, Dan Marino, Jim Kelly, and Steve Young waiting in the wings.

In 2008, there were Peyton Manning, Tom Brady injured on opening day, and Brett Favre on his last legs.

The game has changed, and the supply of brilliant, Hall of Fame–caliber quarterbacks has not kept up.

"The system does not allow for the development of a quarterback," says Doug Williams, who won the Super Bowl with the Redskins. "He is either good right now or he isn't. Occasionally a player may have a chance to go someplace else to get his chance, but we either push them into a starting role before they are ready or we don't give them a chance to mature in a system."

There are myriad reasons for this. One is that authority has been taken out of the hands of quarterbacks. It started with Paul Brown, and later Tom Landry, sending in plays from the sidelines. It continued with scripting—which took the managing of the ebb and flow of the game off the field and into the coaches' booth. Next came a narrowing of options on audibles. And finally we had a generation of quarterbacks coming up who had *never* called their own plays. Some, when given the opportunity, turned out to be quite gifted at it (Tom Brady, for example). Others never got the hang of the rough art.

"In 1957 I called every play as a rookie," said Sonny Jurgensen. "Nowadays it has become a coaches' game, but we are getting back to it being a players' game with the Peyton Mannings and Tom Bradys of the world. One coach recently told me that the main reason coaches have to call it is because they need to know the play called so they can evaluate it better."

Jurgensen has an idea to solve that problem: "How about let the quarterback call the play, then let him signal the goddamn thing to *you*?"

You can talk about ice water in the veins and unflappability in the huddle, you can wax eloquent about the steel-blue gaze in Joe Montana's eyes and the slouchy self-assuredness of Namath in his heyday. But in the end, all leadership eventually stems from production. I have known many quarterbacks with the intelligence and charisma to draw people to their leadership who eventually failed because they could not produce on the field. You like them, you wanted to follow them, but the lack of production left you knowing they would lead, but no one would follow. Others may not have had the same natural gifts of leadership, but their ability to produce on the field raised their stature to the point that people just naturally followed. Bill Cowher said of Ben Roethlisberger, "In his rookie year the players liked Ben but it was not like they were naturally drawn to him as their leader." The Steelers actually started Tommy Maddox that season, but Roethlisberger was thrust into the lineup when Maddox was knocked out for the year by my Baltimore Ravens.

"Ben had no command presence in the huddle at all," says Cowher. "I don't think he could identify any of his teammates in the huddle because he had his nose buried in his wristband trying to call each play being piped into his helmet from the offensive coordinator. But he produced at a level that demanded the respect of his teammates, and his ability to lead came from that." The Steelers' only loss that regular season was that game in Baltimore when we knocked Maddox out and Roethlisberger came in. He went on to complete 66 percent of his passes and showed an uncanny ability to make plays outside the design of the offense, and make big plays down the field, consistently throwing fewer than twenty-five passes a game. If I had known Roethlisberger was going to be such a great player I would have ordered my players not to put a finger on Maddox.

Like Flacco for the Ravens in 2008, it was never the intention of the Steelers to play their rookie quarterback so early. And in both cases, the unexpected move that thrust the rookie into action only served to accelerate the experience of the players who would become the franchise quarterbacks in Pittsburgh and Baltimore.

Even though someone else may be calling the plays, the quarterback is still considered the field general by fans and teammates alike—which is why Carson Palmer gets heat for Chad Johnson's meltdowns, and Terrell Owens's antics in Dallas led to criticism of Tony Romo.

I learned this firsthand from having the privilege of working with Hall of Fame quarterback Warren Moon. Moon came to us in Minnesota in 1994 after an incredibly productive career in Houston. They had decided Moon was over the hill and that their new young quarterback, Cody Carlson, was the wave of the future (Carlson started for the Oilers in 1994 but was hurt and never played in the league again).

Warren had a striking presence that demanded respect. My star receiver at the time was Cris Carter. Cris is, in my opinion, the best slot receiver in the history of the game and one of the most gifted athletes I have ever been around. Cris is also known for some of his antics as a wide receiver—maybe the precursor of things to come with temperamental wideouts. Many people misunderstood Cris and thought he was selfish for wanting every ball thrown his way. They didn't understand that it wasn't selfishness; he sincerely believed in his heart that he was open on virtually every play and would be able to catch anything that was thrown to him. Usually, he was right.

Early in their relationship we were playing a game when Cris thought he was open and Warren threw the ball elsewhere. Cris waved his arms down the field and went through some gyrations after the play, exhibiting his frustration that the ball wasn't thrown his way.

Cris knew not to go after someone like Warren, so instead he made a beeline for me on the sideline and let me and everyone else in the stadium know that he had been open. Warren walked up to us, pausing just long enough to calmly inform Cris, "If you ever pull a stunt like that again and embarrass me, I will bury you in this offense and you will never see the ball again."

As good an athlete as Cris was, he was also one of the smartest players I have ever been around. He got the message and never put Warren in that position again.

Then there's the importance of environment: Quarterbacks develop differently in different systems, and a quarterback's brilliance can be stifled by the wrong setup. Archie Manning may have been every bit as good a quarterback and leader as his two Super Bowl–winning sons, but nobody was going to win many games with the New Orleans Saints of the seventies. That wasn't a career; it was a death sentence. In the same manner, Tom Brady never would have won three Super Bowls if he had been drafted in the sixth round by the Detroit Lions rather than the New England Patriots.

This has always been the case. Some quarterbacks don't bloom until they find the right setting. Len Dawson languished for five years on the bench in the NFL of the late fifties and early sixties, completely losing his polish and touch. Then he went to the AFL and found a coach in Hank Stram who could maximize his potential. Over the next eight seasons, he won three AFL championships and a Super Bowl for the Kansas City Chiefs, fashioning a Hall of Fame career from the scrap heap. Jim Plunkett was left for dead after washing out with New England and San Francisco in the seventies, then won two Super Bowls with Oakland.

Here's a good way to start a bar fight: Ask ten people to list the top ten quarterbacks of all time. Even among football people, you'd come up with a composite list of thirty to forty names. If you asked a GM, coach, owner, writer, or fan to list the one thing that made each one great, you would find an even wider and more varied perspective: the nimble pocket presence of Joe Montana, the quick release of Dan Marino, the mechanical precision of Troy Aikman, the athleticism of Steve Young, the intelligence of Peyton Manning, the total command of Tom Brady, the toughness of Terry Bradshaw.

There are twenty-three "modern era" quarterbacks in the Hall of Fame, ranging from Otto Graham, Y. A. Tittle, Bob Waterfield, Norm Van Brocklin, and Bobby Layne in the forties and fifties, to Johnny Unitas, Sonny Jurgensen, Fran Tarkenton, Roger Staubach, Bart Starr, Joe Namath, Len Dawson, Terry Bradshaw, and Bob Griese in the sixties into the seventies. After that come John Elway, Steve Young, Joe Montana, Warren Moon, Dan Marino, Dan Fouts, Jim Kelly, and Troy Aikman.

We have to be careful about judging past greats by present standards. In the sixties and seventies, passing was a higher-risk, higher-reward proposition, with lower leaguewide completion percentages and higher rates of pass interceptions. With six Super Bowl rings between them, Terry Bradshaw and John Elway would top the "rocket arm" division of great quarterbacks. In Elway's brilliant seventeen-year career he cracked the 60 percent completion mark only three times. Bradshaw never once in his career completed 60 percent of his passes on the year, and was a career 51 percent passer. The legendary Johnny Unitas never completed 60 percent of his passes. Joe Namath was rarely above 50 percent in a given year, and threw 173 touchdowns compared to 220 interceptions.

Joe Montana, on the other hand, had only two years in his fifteen-year Hall of Fame career where he was under 60 percent. Peyton Manning and Tom Brady have been under 60 percent only once in their careers, both times when they were rookies. Arm strength has always been coveted in the NFL, as displayed by consistently hitting the out route or firing it in on the quick post. But since the advent of the West Coast Offense, that perspective has changed. Even the ability to throw the deep ball is more a question of timing than of arm strength.

You could probably identify a single aspect of each of these quarterbacks' games to which many would attribute their success. To some degree each possessed a combination of functional intelligence, athletic ability, arm strength, toughness, and command presence. But each had these attributes in different combinations that worked singularly for them. One Hall of Famer's mixture of skills varies from that of the next, and each mixture is impossible to duplicate. You either have the right, rare winning combination of abilities in the right time and place, or you don't.

Bill Walsh, in his usual outside-the-box perspective, used the analogy of the concert pianist. "Any person who knows how to read music and play the piano has the same basic skills as the most accomplished concert pianist. The difference is the truly unique combination of skill, passion, focus, competitiveness, and dedication that separates one from the other." These are the same attributes it takes to play quarterback in the National Football League and the hardest to isolate, identify, and quantify.

But find me a tough gym rat with a live arm, pinpoint control, and a level head, and I'll take my chances.

SHOTGUN SOLO RIGHT CLOSE Z LEFT 2 JET RATTLE Y DRAG

There was a time when offenses were simple. The Green Bay Packers of the 1960s ran essentially nine plays, with little variation. The Miami Dolphins of the seventies weren't much more complex, running through their thin offensive playbook with remorseless efficiency, overpowering the opposition at the point of attack, relying on a disciplined offensive line to open holes for their bulldozing running backs, and wearing down opponents physically over four quarters.

As recently as Super Bowl IV, in 1970, the Minnesota Vikings used only two basic offensive formations and did not run a single play with a shift or a man in motion. In that era, even teams that passed usually did so with a minimum of deception. The "vertical" offense of the Raiders of the seventies used a massive offensive line that could both run-block and pass-protect with equal skill, then employed superior outside speed to free their receivers for big plays.

But the days of simplistic black-and-white offensive schemes are long gone. "Brown Right 38" has given way to "Shotgun

Solo Right Close Z Left 2 Jet Rattle Y Drag." Modern football is a complex mix of trickery and misdirection, of shifts and motion and disguises, all coming at a faster pace than they did a generation ago.

You can go all the way back to the old American Football League of the 1960s and see the antecedents of modern offenses in the way that Sid Gillman put receivers all over the field, and in the complex alignments and shifts and motion employed by Hank Stram.

But the seeds of the modern game, and twenty-first-century offenses, were planted in Cincinnati, Ohio, in 1970. The expansion Cincinnati Bengals, owned and coached by the legendary Paul Brown, lost their young quarterback Greg Cook to an injury that would ultimately end his career. With Cook and his extraordinary skill set out of the picture, the Bengals were left with backup Virgil Carter, a gritty quarterback with a below-average arm and above-average smarts.

Realizing he would have to retool the offense around his second-string quarterback and an inexperienced offensive line, Brown turned to his offensive assistant, Bill Walsh, to come up with a plan. Walsh, as much out of necessity as any revolutionary vision, installed an offense that could work with the personnel at hand. Though Carter couldn't drill the ball on deep patterns, he was accurate on short and intermediate routes, and the Bengals' running backs were unusually nimble, with soft hands, able to catch passes out of the backfield with more dexterity than most of the bull-rushing contemporaries of the era.

Walsh shortened the standard drop that Carter would take, from seven steps to three or five, hoping his smallish offensive line could hold blocks for that compressed period. He put more running backs into passing patterns, opening up the field horizontally. With his excellent tight end, Bob Trumpy, he started running more drag routes, having Trumpy "chip" (football terminology for a move that is more of a bump than an outright block) a defender at the line of scrimmage, then sneak across the field underneath the linebackers' or strong safety's coverage.

While passing targets were spreading out the field, Carter's progressive reads were simplified, so that his first two or three options were usually within a smaller range of vision, on one side of the field. Walsh also began "scripting" the opening series before each game, giving his head coach and players an early look at their initial plan of attack.

The genesis of scripting came with the breakfasts that Walsh and Brown would share on game days. The old coach wasn't spending the time to do the hard detail work of game-planning, but he was still fascinated with Walsh's agile mind and would frequently ask for Walsh's "openers." At the time Bill would present his complete plan for key situations in the game and the opening sequences he planned to use on "base" down and distances (which is to say, situations in which the down-and-distance combination were within a normal range: first and ten, second and medium, third and short; in atypical situations, such as second and one, or third and twenty-two, he would be more likely to go off the script). After a while it occurred to Bill that he could do the same thing the night before with his players to give them the same "heads-up" he was providing for Brown.

The effect was nearly instantaneous. The modestly talented Bengals won a division title in their third year of existence. Even when they stumbled a year later, Carter's completion percentage rose from 51 percent to 62 percent. This was the birth of what eventually became known as the West Coast Offense. In later years Walsh would observe, "We had no idea that we were creating a template for the future of offense in the NFL. We did what we did just to stay competitive, then expanded on it as we continued to have success."

In 1979, Walsh became the head coach of the San Francisco 49ers, as inept a franchise as there was in pro football in the late seventies, and set about putting the same principles in place. By the time he made it to his third season in San Francisco, he'd assembled a champion. His offensive line was smart, mobile, and disciplined. His corps of receivers included such excellent receiving running backs as Roger Craig and Tom Rathman, and the reliable wideout Dwight Clark. And he had a young, athletic quarterback out of Notre Dame named Joe Montana, who was blessed with an otherworldly vision of the geometry of the field that allowed him to spot receivers seemingly even before they came open. (Marcus Allen, who would play in the same backfield as Montana late in their respective careers in Kansas City, once said, "Watching him work the two-minute drill is like looking over the shoulder of an artist as he completes a fine painting. He never gets rattled, never shows concern. There is about him an attitude that is unbelievably contagious.")

By 1980, the script of Walsh's opening plays had grown from five plays to twenty-five plays, allowing his team to visualize days before the game how they'd attack their opposition. By the time it matured in San Francisco, Walsh's offense seemed to be a step or two ahead of its opposition, able to set the tone of the game, take full advantage of the liberalized passing rules, and keep the defense off-balance. The seminal moment for the evolution of the West Coast Offense and the validation of Walsh's theories may have come in the fourteenth game of the 1980 season, the year before the 49ers won their first Super

Bowl. Down 35–7 at the half, Montana rallied his team to tie the game, 35–35, before winning it on a long drive in overtime.

The next season, the 49ers blossomed. They also broke away from the heavy influence that the Dallas Cowboys exerted on that era. "America's Team" was the most imitated club in football during the seventies. The Cowboys used computerized scouting, and the rest of the league eventually followed suit. The Cowboys used a multiple offense with lots of shifts; so the rest of the league used multiple offenses with lots of shifts. The Cowboys based much of their defensive philosophy on computer-generated tendencies identified from an opponent's previous games; so the rest of league based much of their defensive philosophy on computer-generated tendencies identified from an opponent's previous games.

But Walsh's twenty-five-play script subverted all of that. You couldn't plan for the 49ers because the 49ers didn't have an identifiable set of biases on first or second down, and they possessed such versatile running backs that they were equally effective running or passing on third down.

A generation later, Walsh's ideas can be seen at every level of the game. It's true that no team runs a pure version of Walsh's West Coast Offense today. (I have often asked friends around the league to define the West Coast Offense, and most of them are hard-pressed to do so. Most people will concede that if you throw a pass shorter than six yards and have been to Disneyland, you are officially a "West Coast" coach.) But it's also true that Walsh's principles—the short drops, the quick reads, the tendency-proof concept of play-scripting, the widespread use of the tight end as a key weapon in the passing game—have become deeply embedded in the new conventional wisdom of pro football.

Walsh's influence goes way beyond the playbook. My first job in pro football was in San Francisco in 1979, as an assistant publicity director. In 1977, I had been lucky enough to be drafted by the 49ers out of Brigham Young, was quickly cut, got invited to training camp as a free agent by the Cowboys a year later, and was cut again. Walsh hired me, because he felt that the communication between the football players and the publicity department would run more smoothly if there was a former football player with communications experience (my major at Brigham Young) to serve as a go-between.

In this and a dozen other ways, Walsh brought a more thoughtful, compassionate philosophy to bear on running a football team. He wasn't a typical player's coach, not a Dick Vermeil hugs-and-tears type of guy. But without getting too close to his players, Walsh was very aware of the abuses he'd seen elsewhere in the pro game, of old-school coaches who'd belittled their players and caused resentment. And you can see that evolved attitude all over the league today. One small example of Walsh's influence: When former Walsh assistant Mike Holmgren was the head coach in Green Bay in the nineties, he began bringing a black barber in from Milwaukee to cut the hair of African-American players, providing a service he knew they couldn't get in Green Bay.

Another example was the way Walsh delivered criticism. He'd rarely insult a player directly, always give critiques through his assistants. For instance, if a running back didn't use the right technique on pass protection, Bill would walk right past the player and chew out running backs coach Billy Matthews. "Billy, are you going to be able to get this guy to punch with his left hand properly?" he'd ask. "Or do I need to get another coach in here to pass that information on to him in a way that he can use it on the field?" The running back in question would likely feel even worse, after watching his position coach taking heat on his behalf. But that player wasn't being belittled in front of his peers. (The assistants, who were bearing the brunt of Walsh's wrath, understood the larger good that was being accomplished. Nevertheless, it was still hard to take an ass-chewing in front of your players.)

Not all the changes come from coaches and players. One of the least understood influences on the evolution of football is the simplest—the rules of the game. The NFL's Competition Committee, formally established in 1970 and chaired by Cowboys' president Tex Schramm for twenty-five years, was the incubator for ideas and innovations in the way the game was played.

Schramm—joined on the Competition Committee in the seventies by a distinguished group that included Don Shula, Al Davis, and Paul Brown—understood how important offense was to the game's appeal, and as Pete Rozelle's oldest friend in professional football, he had a bias toward promoting scoring and opening up the game.

Nine times out of ten, if not ninety-nine times out of one hundred, what was good for the game of football also turned out to be good for the business of football. The changes made by the Competition Committee, often over the protests of the older guard of the league, have significantly altered the landscape of offensive football and broadened the appeal of the game.

In 1974, the committee moved to reduce the number of field goals, which had increased to a total of nearly three per game the previous season. The goalposts were moved to the back of the end zone and failed kicks attempted outside the twenty-yard line resulted in the opponents' taking possession at the original line of scrimmage rather than the twenty.

More important, the passing game was opened up. Whereas defenders once were allowed an unlimited number of hits on a receiver until the ball was in the air, now they were limited to a single "chuck" on a receiver once he was three yards beyond the line of scrimmage.

In 1978, the committee further limited contact on receivers to one hit, which now had to occur within five yards of the line of scrimmage. From then on, the receiver could not legally be hit until a pass had arrived. Limiting the one hit to within five yards rather than beyond three (the rule in '74) was a subtle change that had broad implications. The bump-and-run of the early seventies was essentially outlawed with this rule, giving way to a greater cushion for prime receivers. Defenses could still choose to play their cornerbacks in press coverage, right up at the line of scrimmage, but if they didn't successfully make their chuck, the receiver would be running free in the pattern.

Defenses soon responded with more zone coverages, but even then, offensive coordinators could now run their patterns with more precision and have greater confidence that a receiver would arrive unobstructed at a specific point in the route. This, in turn, led to more opportunities for tight ends deeper down the field, in the seams of the zone, and for running backs coming out of the backfield, underneath the zone coverage. Within three seasons, passing plays rose from 38 to 47 percent of the total number of offensive plays, and scoring increased by nearly a touchdown a game overall. (This eventually led to a change in defensive philosophy, as defenses responded with a more gambling style that can be seen today. But more about that in the next chapter.)

In 1994, the two-point conversion, used for decades in college football, and in the sixties in the American Football League, was added. Kicking tees were also reduced in height from three inches to one inch, and the kickoff line was moved back from the thirty-five- to the thirty-yard line.

The effect of those rules was to make the game more wide-open, both strategically and literally. In the sixties and seventies, the days of the classic, two-back offense, nine of the eleven players on offense were all within five to seven yards of the ball at the line of scrimmage. Now that has changed. Three- and four-receiver sets have spread the game out to all fifty-three horizontal yards of the field. And even the quarterback is moving away from the center. The percentage of snaps that NFL offenses run out of the shotgun has nearly doubled over the past five seasons, from 17.3 percent in 2004 to 34.1 percent in 2008.

There is plenty of disagreement in coaching circles over the utility of the shotgun. Bill Walsh held it in disdain, believing it put limitations on the running game and play-action fakes. Some quarterbacks, like Drew Brees of the Saints, are on record saying they don't like it because it forces them to take their eyes off the secondary as the ball is snapped. But the standard shotgun—with one running back offset in the backfield next to the quarterback—has become a staple in third-and-long situations, since it gets the quarterback back to pass more quickly and allows running backs staying in for protection to better pick up blitzing linebackers coming through gaps.

The added emphasis on passing has changed the composition of the eleven men on the field. Fullbacks—squat, solidly built running backs whose primary duty was to be an additional blocker on running plays—were once a staple of every offense, but they might be going the way of pay phones and videocassettes, relics of a not-so-distant past. In today's game most teams will carry only one true fullback, if that. Perhaps no player in today's game exemplifies the position more than Lorenzo Neal, a sixteen-year veteran and four-time Pro Bowler. For each of the past eleven seasons, he has been the lead blocker for a running back who surpassed one thousand rushing yards.

"My definition is 'mood changer,'" he says of his role. "If you have the skill, you can be the glue of the offense," he says. "By that I mean that, well, if I go one on one against a linebacker, my mentality is that he's not going to be thinking about making this tackle. I won't let him. He's going to be thinking about *me*."

The problem is that running a fullback-oriented offense is not a sometime kind of proposition. It is hard to integrate this physical style of play in today's game. The big chunks of yardage that are required to move the ball in today's NFL require a roster of wide receivers, tight ends, and running backs who have the skills needed to expand on the passing game.

The phase-out began in the eighties, when Joe Gibbs developed the "H-back"—a taller, more agile player than most fullbacks, who retained blocking skills and could also be a receiving threat—who was deployed in the Redskins' run-heavy attack. By 2006, when the Indianapolis Colts won the Super Bowl, the team didn't have a single true fullback on its roster.

Today's H-backs are closer to tight ends than fullbacks, and the popularity of three and four wide-receiver sets has led to more "Ace" formations in which only one running back is in the backfield.

Among the fraternity of coaches, Gibbs would comment on how the tight end was a player that you were always half pissed off at. Either he was big and physical enough to be a good point-of-attack blocker, but obviously not much of a threat in the passing game, or he was another extension of the wide receiver corps with great matchup potential against the slower linebackers and safeties, but a terrible run blocker.

When the new round of head coaches, many of them former defensive coordinators, hit the scene in the late eighties, they all had the same mantra: Play good defense and run the ball well. The league has always coveted a good running game in general and a good running back in particular. However, three things have become clear in the past fifteen years that have altered the way we view running backs: First, in terms of injury risk, it is the most perilous position in football, not only because running backs are subject to so many hits, but because even a slight injury, one that other position players would and could play through, can greatly hinder a running back's speed and effectiveness. Second, running the ball has not necessarily been the cornerstone of championship teams; even running-based teams that won titles didn't do so *because* of their running game, and the 2000 Ravens are a shining example of that. Third, it's become clear that you don't have to spend a high draft choice to get a good one.

No position takes more of a beating than running back. The benchmark for an "every down" back who could command the highest salary is someone who carries three hundred plus times a year, or nearly twenty times a game. Yet research clearly shows that when a workhorse running back has consecutive three-hundred-carry seasons, the cumulative toll it takes on his body almost guarantees that his effectiveness will soon be reduced to the point where a team won't want to give him that many touches. Shaun Alexander is a prototypical example. The nineteenth overall pick out of Alabama for the Seattle Seahawks in 2000, Alexander played sparingly in his rookie season, then began a string of five consecutive years in which he carried the ball at least 295 times per season. In 2005 he led the NFL in rushing with 370 carries and 1,880 yards, leading his team to the Super Bowl, which they lost to the Pittsburgh Steelers. The next spring Alexander received a new eight-year, $62 million contract with a $15 million signing bonus and adorned the cover of Madden 2006. But he missed part of the next two seasons with injury, wasn't re-signed after 2007, and wasn't picked up by any other team until October 2008, when the Redskins brought him on as a backup to Clinton Portis. After averaging 4.9 yards per carry the last two seasons before the contract, Alexander averaged just 3.5 per carry the next two years.

Once a back is viewed as damaged goods, his value in the market plummets precipitously. Rather than run the risk of overusing a single back, many teams in the NFL—including 2008 champion Pittsburgh and contenders Arizona, the New York Giants, Tennessee, and the Baltimore Ravens—have taken to using a running-back-by-committee approach.

For all the talk about rushing winning championships, there are facts that fly directly in the face of that belief. Only twice has the league's top rushing team (the Dolphins in 1972 and the Bears in 1985) gone on to win the Super Bowl. Half the Super Bowl champions of the past ten years have been in the bottom half of the team rushing rankings.

A number of good backs have been drafted in the upper half of the first round recently, including Adrian Peterson, Jonathan Stewart, and Marshawn Lynch. But several teams excelled in 2008 with lower-round backs: Steve Slaton was drafted in the third round by Houston and produced over twelve hundred yards rushing and fifty receptions. Second-round pick Matt Forte was the first rookie running back since Walter Payton to start for the Chicago Bears; he produced nearly half of the Bears' yards from scrimmage in 2008. Kevin Smith, a third-round choice of the Lions, accounted for more than twelve hundred yards rushing and receiving.

Running backs who can block and catch out of the backfield

have proven to be a more valued commodity than ever before. The formula most popular today calls for a lead back, who is kept under three hundred carries, a solid backup who is good for one hundred carries a season, and possibly a third back to serve as a third-down specialist and adept receiver.

The evolution of the game also has dictated that some teams' personnel departments have now divided tight end into two distinct positions, one being the sleek, deep-seam receiving threat (like Tony Gonzalez, Kellen Winslow Jr., and Antonio Gates) and the other being the big, hulking grinder (essentially a sixth offensive lineman) who often serves as the extra blocker at the point of attack on running plays. Other teams make the same distinction between deep-threat wideouts and better-blocking possession receivers, who often play in the slot on three-wideout sets.

And if an offense has versatile players at the key "swing" positions—especially tight end—the play caller can make it extremely difficult for the defense to guess right. When Dick Vermeil's scoreboard-busting Chiefs of the early 2000s were at their most potent, many teams routinely put a cornerback on Tony Gonzalez, trying to cover him on deeper routes. But when the Chiefs used Gonzalez as a blocker aiding their superb offensive line, the defense had one fewer linebacker and one extra cornerback trying to face such future Hall of Famers as Willie Roaf and Will Shields on sweeps, with running backs Priest Holmes and Larry Johnson often not encountering contact until they were five yards past the line of scrimmage.

But players with that kind of versatility are rare. So what coaches do more often is rotate personnel to keep defenses off-balance. In Green Bay in the nineties, Mike Holmgren expanded on Bill Walsh's scripting by varying plays but also personnel groups. This meant that beyond the quarterback and five offensive lineman, the rest of the offensive alignment could vary significantly from one play to the next. Holmgren's idea, perfectly articulated with his Packers teams of the nineties, was to keep the defense off-balance and dictate the tempo of the game.

Here's one example of a team's typical variations. Remember that the first six offensive players—five interior linemen and a quarterback—are a given:

Formation	WR	TE	RB
Base	2	1	2
H-back	2	1	1 (plus the H-back)
Trips	3	1	1
4 wides	4	0	1
Empty	4	1	0

Defenses can and do study tendencies within each of these different offensive packages, but adjusting to them in the real time of the game calls for a lot of shuttling on defense as well.

Offensive minds like Sean Payton and Mike Martz will tell you that they like being able to dictate to the defenses the pace of the game rather than the other way around. "Most defenses like to carry multiple packages into a game based on a couple of offensive personnel groups," says Payton. "This will be made up of different pressures and coverages based on down and distance. The more personnel groups you can roll through, the larger the number of packages the defense has to carry to deal with it. There comes a point where they just can't deal with it all and thus cut down on the packages they will try to run."

Martz points out that this philosophy lends itself to finding specific roles for players who might not otherwise be able to contribute. "Like the H-back, there are backs and receivers that might not have the physical tools to be an every-down player but do have skills that can be very important to an offense in a very specific role, players like [wide receivers] Ricky Proehl and Brandon Stokely." In a sixteen-year career, Proehl played for six different teams, including Martz's insanely productive offenses in St. Louis in the heyday of the "Greatest Show on Turf."

With all these personnel groupings now at their disposal, most teams in the NFL fall into one of two general play-calling philosophies.

- "Call." These teams make a call in the huddle, then follow it up with shifts or motion at the line of scrimmage to increase the chances of the play's working. Payton's New Orleans Saints and Jim Zorn's Washington Redskins are excellent examples of this philosophy. This style also readily fits with the "scripted" forms of offense, in that they offer a readily programmable set of plays. As Mike Martz is fond of pointing out, "When you have this as your base offense it doesn't matter what they run. You only have to focus on what you run and how you execute."

  This was the model for the Super Bowl XL–winning Steelers. Teams that fit this profile usually audible only against specific defensive alignments. The ultimate control here rests with the offensive coordinator, and success with this style depends on his ability to adequately anticipate how a defense will respond to a specific personnel group, alignment, and shift.

- "Check." This is a more fluid system made possible by talented quarterbacks like Peyton Manning and Tom Brady. In the check system, teams line up in a more or less static formation, and then let the quarterback look at the defense and select the best run or pass available. The control here rests with the quarterback, and success depends on his ability to sense—in the moment and on the field—the best play to call against a heavily camouflaged defense.

In the first style, there is less flexibility on the part of the quarterback, and much emphasis is placed on shifting players or putting them in motion to reveal whether the defense is playing zone or man coverage. The emphasis is on quick calls, quick shifts and motion, and playing fast, so that the defense has to respond to a series of quick changes and can never get fully comfortable.

If it seems like the second style, putting control back in the hands of the quarterback, is a reaction against virtually every trend of offensive football in the past generation, that's because it is. For decades, control on offense flowed away from the quarterback and off the field. But as defenses responded with more disguised coverages and zone blitzes, it became necessary for the offense to make more adjustments right up to the snap.

Coaches who find quarterbacks who can reliably make the right decisions in the moment have a big advantage in anticipating what audibles to call for certain looks. Manning and Brady have been coaches on the field. But it's the rare quarterback who has shown this sort of aptitude.

Tom Moore, the longtime offensive coordinator and architect of the Indianapolis Colts system, loves the simplicity of the system. "This does not require a large inventory of plays because it lets the quarterback access what he wants when he wants it. Most plays require a steep learning curve for players to adapt what they have to do versus different looks. It requires a great deal of time in the classroom identifying those looks and then a great deal of practice time to work against the multiple looks they might face. In fact you rarely get a chance to run your players through all the variations they might see. This way you are only running the plays you want and are comfortable with them against the looks you want."

Obviously, this system puts a premium on the quarterback's ability to execute it. Quarterbacks like Peyton Manning and Tom Brady have had record success with such systems and have proven to be incredibly durable as well. When either has been hurt, as was the case in 2008 in New England when Tom Brady blew out his knee on Kickoff Weekend, it was not just a matter of plugging in the next guy. The Patriots' system had to be modified to account for the inexperience and the more limited skills of their backup, Matt Cassel.

In 2008, we also saw an example of how a team may change its philosophy because of the unique talents of its personnel. Eric Mangini, in his first two years with the New York Jets, ran a system that was very much a "call" system. With the well-publicized acquisition of Brett Favre the Jets knew they would have to adapt their system to accommodate the "check" capabilities of their new, legendary QB.

One element that splits the difference between the two is the "kill" audible system, which relies on presnap reads but is not as freewheeling as those employed by the Colts and Patriots. In the kill system, a quarterback will call two plays in the huddle, connecting them with a word indicating that the one that is run will depend on the defense that is employed. An example might be "Spread Right, Kill, 40 Gut to Quick 2 Jet Dragon." This is a simple inside zone run that will "kill," or switch, to an equally simple slant-flat route combination should the defense deploy a hard eight-man run-stopping front. When the quarterback comes to the line, he can either run the primary call or "kill" to the other play.

You can "kill" an inside run to an outside run, a weak-side play to a strong-side play, a run to a pass, or vice versa. This style of offense brings just a little more focus to the players and gives them specific options to rely on in the check game. Though an arm injury ruined his 2008 season, Carson Palmer and the Cincinnati Bengals have taken this "kill" audible game to a very productive level. "I like the offense because it gives me a great deal of latitude to get to a play that has a higher degree of probability to succeed, but doesn't put the burden of calling the entire offense on me on any given play," he says.

One of the downsides to a pure "check" or audible system is that it tends to run very quickly and puts a team's defense back on the field more quickly than coaches would prefer. Even sustained drives don't take as much time as they do in a system in which the offense huddles before each play. The "kill" system allows the quarterback to control the tempo a little better.

Styles change, formations and packages go in and out of fashion. But one commodity has remained unchanged for the past half century in pro football: the irreversible push toward speed.

From the huddle to the snap of the ball, much more is happening. And once the ball is snapped, everything happens much faster than it did a generation ago. Speed is the defining factor of the modern game. The slender difference between an All-Pro left tackle and a pedestrian one can often be as simple as the ability to react in half an eye blink (rather than a full one) to an outside rush. Defenses are faster than ever before, and that means offenses must account for that speed. Although the prototype physique for all positions is larger than it was a generation ago, it's the speed on defense that has kept the game from being overrun by four-hundred-pound offensive linemen. In the twenty-first century, big isn't enough; you have to be mobile and quick as well.

It's not just the players that are faster—it's also the reads, the drops, the time that offensive lines can protect the quarterback. Ask any rookie about his first experience of NFL football and the answer is invariably the same: the speed at which the game is played is not just different from that of college ball but dramatically so. Kevin Smith, the rookie running back for the Detroit Lions, marveled, "In college when you get into the second level down the field on a big run you expect to have to deal with a safety or corner. In this league, heck, you get run down by some defensive lineman."

Take a look at the evolution of the humble screen pass. It was run in the nineties in a way quite similar to the way it was run in the sixties. But now there are multiple variations to the screen pass. The dart screen (also known as the kick screen) develops more rapidly, while the wide receiver screen—used extensively in the modern spread offenses in college, and more recently adapted at the NFL level—uses the slot receiver as an outside blocker, who seals the outside cornerback while the wide receiver receiving the screen loops inside.

The speed of the game is tougher on the quarterback than any other position. The Atlanta Falcons' young signal caller Matt Ryan showed a great deal of maturity in being able to identify what the speed of the game means to the quarterback position. Ryan said, "I have heard the saying that for quarterbacks it is about when the game 'slows down.' I don't know about it ever slowing down. It looks pretty fast to me. But I do think as I gain more experience that I will begin to recognize things more quickly and be able to make quicker and better decisions. That's maybe what they are talking about."

Not all of the influences on the game come from within. In 2002, University of California–Berkeley professor David Romer published a paper using business models to evaluate NFL teams' tendencies on fourth down. Based on data from over seven hundred games, Romer concluded that teams tended to be far too conservative about play-calling in fourth-down situations, especially close to an opponent's goal line.

It's impossible to evaluate how much influence Romer's study has, and certain coaches dismissed the entire paper as the irrelevant conclusions of an egghead who knew nothing of football. At the same time, he made a compelling intellectual case that the risk-to-benefit ratio on fourth down usually argued for bolder strategy. The study sampled over twenty-six hundred fourth-down plays, concluding that in 41 percent of those cases, offenses would have been justified in going for it. In fact, the teams in question went for it on only 4 percent of those plays.

Most coaches I know granted Romer his central point, while observing that the business model didn't allow for factors such as confidence, momentum, media criticism, and specific matchups against varying opponents. The number of instances of a team's going for it on fourth-down attempts steadily increased in the NFL since 2004, from just over fourteen per team per season in 2004 to nearly seventeen per team per season in 2007, then dipped back down to fifteen in 2008.

(Romer's work is the tip of the iceberg. One of the big changes in the last decade has been a much more widespread and effective effort to quantify the game statistically, providing a football equivalent to the sabermetric revolution that rocked baseball over the past twenty-five years. *The Hidden Game of Football,* by Bob Carroll, Pete Palmer, John Thorn, and David Pietrusza, first published in 1988, was the seminal book in the field, and in the twenty-first century, the work done by FootballOutsiders .com, publishers of the annual *Pro Football Prospectus,* has shed a great deal of light on aspects of the game that had been under-reported—or completely inaccurately reported—in the past.)

Offenses are also opening up in other ways. Though the full package of college spread offenses hasn't been widely used in the NFL, there has been more use of variations on the shotgun set, with more direct snaps to running backs, a relic of the old single-wing formation. In 2008, the most successful of these variations was the "Wildcat" formation used by the Miami Dolphins, with quarterback Chad Pennington split out wide as a receiver, and running back Ronnie Brown taking the deep snap from the center.

There are reasons to suspect that the use of Wildcat types of packages is more than a passing fad. From Kordell "Slash" Stewart to Antwaan Randle-El to Hines Ward, the Steelers have been using players in hybrid backfield positions for more than a decade. That could mean an All-Pro running back with some passing skills—a new type of back.

But the tenets of the modern game—a lot of different personnel packages, a lot of shifts and motion, a lot of things for the defenses to chart and prepare for, a lot of misdirection for the defenses to get through—will not change.

One other thing won't change: No matter what offenses do, no matter how innovative offensive coordinators get, the defenses will *always* catch up. They may have to take more risks to do so, but sooner or later, they find a way to account for virtually every offensive innovation that exists. That's an essential part of the game as well.

"SOMEBODY'S BAND IS GOING TO PLAY"

Every year the NFL has a coaches' subcommittee meeting in which the league's Competition Committee consults with the league's head coaches on changes that are being considered.

Not long after I started attending these meetings, I figured out the tone that all of them would take. A representative of the Competition Committee, typically one of the head coaches serving on the main committee, would come in and explain the latest rule change that would be put in. Inevitably, the committee's proposed changes would help the offense. The offensive guys like me would smile—"They're *finally* going to enforce the wording of defensive pass interference? About time!"—while the head coaches from defensive backgrounds would sit there fuming, smoke coming out of their ears, as they contemplated the latest way that the committee was going to screw them.

A few years back I was sitting next to Carolina Panthers head coach John Fox, who listened patiently to the latest round of rule changes and, at one point, interrupted and said, "You know what? How about if we just played with ten guys on defense? Would that be easier? Would you guys like that?"

That's the defensive personality in a nutshell: determined, sardonic, slightly paranoid, and always ready for combat.

You learn when you become an NFL head coach that you are no longer an offensive or defensive coach. A head coach can't limit his perspective and thinking to that type of isolated view or he's likely to find himself quickly going back to a coordinator's job, because he won't last as a head coach very long. Having said that, it is hard not to revert to one's upbringing and view the game through that lens of offense or defense. I found myself doing it at times, even though in Baltimore I had one of the great defenses in NFL history.

So while my background is on the offensive side of things, I understand the defensive coaches' frustration. Almost every major rule change of the past thirty-five years has helped the offense. Offensive linemen can extend their hands to block— which is enough of a benefit in and of itself, but it also makes it *much* easier to disguise when they hold. If a defensive lineman does break through and puts pressure on the quarterback, he can't hit him in the head anymore, and has to make sure he gets to him before the pass is thrown, because officiating crews have grown particular—some coaches would say fanatical— about protecting the quarterback after his release. (This is not only for the safety of the players, it's also for the safety of the business; quarterbacks are stars, and stars need to be healthy.) Defensive backs get one hit on a receiver within five yards of the line of scrimmage, and officials are enforcing that rule more strenuously, and the number of fouls called for illegal contact while receivers are in the route have gone up as well.

So how do defenses continue to keep pace?

The same way they always have. By adapting, by studying, by taking advantage of the offensive mind-set and the patterns that virtually all offensive coaches fall into sooner or later. Also, especially in recent years, by being much more aggressive. As offenses grew more precise with their timed patterns and short passing game in the past two decades, defenses realized they could no longer sit back and wait for a mistake. So they have grown bolder, taken more risks, with more stunts, more safety and corner blitzes, more packages in which five or six or seven players rush.

"We subscribe to the Buddy Ryan school of thought that says, 'You can't be afraid to take a chance and pressure,'" says Browns coach Eric Mangini. "As Buddy used to say, 'Somebody's band is going to play.'"

That's defensive football in the twenty-first century.

But this is getting ahead of the story. Oftentimes, the history of football strategy is presented as a static story of offensive innovations and defensive reactions. In reality, the innovations often come on the defensive side of the ball.

Even as recently as the mid-nineties, there was not a tremendous amount of presnap shifting in NFL offenses. A lot of teams were imitating Bill Walsh's West Coast Offense, without the imagination or the personnel of the original. Many of the teams that were doing so relied on a series of easy reads, and on clear passing lanes—especially on shallow routes—in which to hit their receivers.

Then, in the first half of the nineties, Bill Cowher's Steelers, with legendary defensive coordinator Dick LeBeau, started to popularize the zone blitz, which wreaked havoc with offensive blocking schemes because it brought linebackers and safeties to overload formations, where they hadn't been accounted for, and then put defensive linemen into the shallow zones on coverage, where quarterbacks were least expecting them to pop up. The

Steelers and most other teams that favored the zone blitz typically employed 3–4 sets.

The genius of the zone blitz was that it could frustrate the quarterback and mess with the timing of the entire offense. With linebackers and safeties coming from unexpected places, there were frequent instances when quarterbacks would need to make "hot reads," passing to a receiver who intentionally cut his route short to provide an antidote to the rush. But when linemen were dropping into the very zones where the hot routes might be thrown, offenses were faced with a choice between eating the football and taking a big loss or throwing it anyway and risking a turnover. The "zone blitz" itself was often a misnomer, since it frequently rushed just three or four defenders, but did so from odd positions and angles.

In 1995, in Carolina, head coach Dom Capers and defensive coordinator Vic Fangio did the same thing as the Steelers, but with fewer stars. They rode talent that was good but not great to an NFC Championship Game berth in the franchise's second year of existence.

Dom Capers was particularly creative with bringing corners off the backside edge, from an area you just did not anticipate them coming. When I was with the Vikings, Robert Smith, our explosive running back, was outstanding at starting a play one way then cutting back across the grain and exploding out of the backside. One week when we were playing the Panthers, Robert made one of his patented cuts and the Panthers' defense overcommitted—except for the backside corner, who was blitzing. When Robert cut back, he saw nothing but green grass (well, nothing but green AstroTurf); then he got blown up on a vicious hit by the backside corner. He came off the field and asked, "Who got me? I thought they had overrun the gap." When I told him it was a blitzing cornerback, he responded, "No, really! Who got me?"

Very quickly, offenses began to adjust. People like Joe Gibbs and Mike Martz began recognizing that using multiple personnel groupings, and shifting and motioning of personnel, could give fits to defenses that were becoming more and more exotic about bringing pressure. By changing the strength of the formations (by shifting the tight end or overloading one side or the other with multiple receivers), an offense could change the strength of its protection, thus influencing the vulnerability of the secondary. The last thing a defensive coordinator wants is to commit to bringing pressure, then find the offense shifting in such a way that it suddenly has enough people to pick up that pressure.

By the late nineties, we had success in Minnesota under Dennis Green using more multiple variations and more motion and finding ways to optimize the pair of All-Pro receivers Cris Carter and Randy Moss. A year later, the St. Louis Rams and "The Greatest Show on Turf" arrived. With the full array of three- and four-wideout sets, multiple personnel packages, a dizzying amount of shifts and motion, and even within that, plenty of peels (in which a player goes into motion from one side of the formation to the other, then turns back in the other direction), the Rams' offense caused more headaches than they would have just by having the fleetest set of wide receivers in captivity. Defenses had to absorb it all. What we've seen in this decade is an across-the-board increase in presnap shifts and motion, as a way to make it more difficult for defenses to get a fix on their assignments.

Of course, you can get so obsessed with the details—*What do they tend to do on third and short? What does this personnel package usually signal? When this receiver goes in the slot on first down, how do they like to use him?*—that you lose sight of the big picture. What was true back in the Middle Ages of pro football, in the fifties and sixties, before offenses became multiple, is still true today: Any team with a defense that can consistently stop the run with the first two lines of defense and pressure the quarterback on passes by rushing just four men will be a force to be reckoned with. Football has always been a game of numbers and angles. It is the coaches' job, on either side of the ball, to constantly try to devise a scheme that does one or more of the following: provide more bodies at the point of attack than the opponent; create favorable angles for their players to do their job; and create the best mismatches they can to put their good people on their opponents' bad ones.

This is obvious, but it's something we keep getting reminded of. When I was coaching the Ravens, I caught myself jumping to conclusions about defenses we'd be facing. Every week, I'd get a report from our scouting department, and it would begin with the different fronts that the defense had shown in the past weeks. Any time I'd get a team with a blizzard of different fronts, I'd shake my head and know I was in for a few long nights' work of film study and planning. Inevitably, though, the team that was doing all those different things was hiding something, some weakness that they were trying to prevent the offense from noticing. That same Carolina team that had gone 12–4 and gotten to the NFC Championship Game in 1996 was, by 1997, getting older and sinking to a 7–9 record. On one play, the Panthers' premier pass rusher Kevin Greene was in a rush position on the far left side, but on the snap sprinted back and around the line to the strong side underneath the flanker curl route. Watching him sprint across the field was almost comical. After the game I asked a Carolina assistant what they were trying to do on that play and his answer was,

"We were just trying to manufacture ways to disrupt your passing attack. We didn't think we could hold up doing that conventionally."

Conversely, if I'd get a scouting report on a team that played only a few basic fronts, I'd think to myself that it would be easier to prepare for that week's game. But just as inevitably, I'd find that the team that didn't offer many different looks didn't *need* to. Those defenses were usually sound and strong.

That's the sort of defense we had in Baltimore when we won the Super Bowl in the 2000 season. Our defense was a marvel to watch; it set the NFL record for fewest points allowed in a sixteen-game season, breaking the 1985 Chicago Bears' mark. It shut out four teams and did not allow a touchdown by six of our opponents. Marvin Lewis, our defensive coordinator and now head coach of the Cincinnati Bengals, did a masterful job of using the unique talents of that unit. Even though Lewis was a Dick LeBeau disciple from his days in Pittsburgh, we were not a particularly complex defense because we didn't have to be. Tackles Tony Siragusa and Sam Adams were two huge but athletic talents who made it nearly impossible to run inside, and equally futile for offensive linemen to get up into the second level of the defense to our future Hall of Fame linebacker Ray Lewis.

The consistent push from the middle, which included tackle Rob Burnett, allowed our two premier rush ends, Michael McCrary and Peter Boulware, to come at the quarterback from both sides. This group allowed us to stuff the run and bring a great deal of pressure on passing plays without having to expose the secondary to a lot of man-to-man coverage. Even when we did, we had two great corners in Duane Starks and Chris McAlister to do it with. And for good measure we had Hall of Famer Rod Woodson roaming the back end at free safety.

But most teams won't be able to dominate in that manner, for the simple reason that they won't be able to assemble that type of talent and, when they do, won't be able to allocate two-thirds of their payroll to the defensive side of the ball to keep it.

There are two main variations to the classic straight-up defense seen in the NFL today. On one side, there's the Cover 2, and its celebrated variation, the Tampa 2, as executed by the Tampa Bay Buccaneers in the 1990s and 2000s under Tony Dungy and Monte Kiffin, and in the 2000s by the Indianapolis Colts under Dungy, and the Bears under Lovie Smith. On the other side are the more high-stakes, more instinctual "attacking" defenses, many of which owe much of their inspiration to Buddy Ryan's 46 defense and his eight-men-in-the-box, high-risk, high-reward philosophy.

The Cover 2 is more cerebral, an attempt at turning football into a matter of geometry and physics. There is instinct in any defense, but Cover 2 is much more about discipline. It also helps that its main architect, Dungy, had a mystical ability to get inside the mind of an offensive coordinator and understand *during the game* what the other side was trying to accomplish, and how. This is a rare gift, one that is much more often commented on (we all pride ourselves on adapting well during the game, but most of us make only modest adjustments) than actually accomplished.

Beyond this, Dungy's system relies on a discipline in which people *don't* always flow to the ball, but instead rely first on maintaining their gap discipline and coverage responsibilities. Some defenders never get comfortable in this system, but those who do find that they can still be aggressive, after they accept their primary areas of responsibility.

"The system relies on the structure rather than the individual," says Lovie Smith, who learned under Dungy and teaches a similar version in Chicago. "You have to be committed to doing your job, which also means you have to be willing to let someone else make the play."

Teams can be fairly successful in the Tampa 2 with relatively less high-priced talent, but they still need an imposing, run-stopping "three-technique" tackle (meaning he typically lines up shaded on the outside shoulder of an offensive guard) minding the B gap between the guard and the tackle (gaps are lettered as they move outward: the A gap is between the center and the guard, B gap between the guard and the tackle, and so forth). Rod Marinelli, longtime defensive line coach for the Tampa Bay Buccaneers and former head coach of the Lions, said, "The three-technique is the piston that drives the engine." An adept three-technique tackle can force the interior part of the offensive line to have to do "extra" things to account for him, while at the same time giving some very quick and verifiable keys to the rest of the front seven. You also need an outstanding rush end, whether it be Dwight Freeney with the Colts or Simeon Rice with the Bucs of the 1990s. The system is at its best only if you can put pressure on the QB with a four-man rush and do not have to commit a good deal more to pressure. Gap and lane integrity is at the heart of the effectiveness of the defense.

Just as essentially, the Tampa 2 requires a fierce-tackling safety who can move down into the box and make the sort of cleat-lifting tackles that get played on highlight shows. If there's an essential player in the Tampa 2, it's that safety—and they're hard to find. Bob Sanders of the Colts is one of the best tacklers in football, but he's relatively small and hits so hard that he often winds up injured. John Lynch played the role with the great Bucs' defenses of the nineties.

• • •

The Cover 2 requires speed throughout the defense, especially at middle linebacker. That player usually has the responsibility to drop deep in coverage (making the name Cover 2 a misnomer, because it's really a Cover 3, with a linebacker instead of a nickel back dropping deep). Even with a fleet linebacker covering deep, it is possible to get down the middle of the defense, the classic vulnerability to most Cover 2s. But that far away from the ball, often twenty or thirty yards downfield, the linebacker doesn't really have to cover the seam receiver closely. It can be enough if he *appears* to have him covered from the quarterback's perspective. The weak-side linebacker is the last part of the equation. More so than any other player, he has to be athletic and a sound open-field tackler. Former Tampa Bay linebacker Derrick Brooks was the ultimate player in this position. Again here, the key is preventing small plays from becoming big plays, and Brooks's ability to come up and minimize the gain of a back who's had the ball dropped off to him was crucial.

Dungy credits Chuck Noll as the one who most shaped his philosophies about defense: speed over size, and placing a priority on only two statistics—points scored and turnovers.

"Be fundamentally sound, don't get beat deep, keep the ball in front of you, and quickly come up and tackle," Dungy says. "At the heart of the system is to build the box when you think they are going to run and play zone when you think they are going to pass. If you can force the quarterback to drop the ball off, and then your guys rally to the tackle, it is very difficult for a team to execute consistently enough with ten- to twelve-play drives to beat you."

Once the ball is caught, the Tampa 2 requires even more

discipline. It's about numbers and angles, about preventing big plays through not just sure tackling, but technically sound tackling, in which players outside the hashmarks are taught to tackle in such a way that even if a receiver does break free, he will be channeled away from the tackler and toward the center of the field, where other tacklers are closing in hot pursuit. When a team has the talent and discipline to execute it, the Tampa 2 can be frustrating to play against. It's not simply that you don't get big gains, you begin after a while to feel that you have *no chance* at big gains.

In the modern game, most teams are playing a more aggressive style, even teams that use a Cover 2 as their main scheme. "We have what we call 'collision point,' where in each defense we know there will be an opportunity to make a hit that will cause a takeaway," says the Bears linebacker Lance Briggs. "We don't call them turnovers. That sounds like we are just waiting for the offense to give us the ball. We want to create a mind-set where we aren't waiting for anything."

Underlying that mind-set is the modern update of the old-school defensive philosophy that says the best defense is one that brings the game to the offense, forces it out of its rhythm, and puts relentless pressure on the quarterback. When this is done well, it can be intimidating to an offense. Pass patterns are less adventuresome, there are fewer receivers out on routes (so that maximum protection can be offered by a tight end or running back), and offenses are acutely aware of needing to develop plays quickly.

One of the foremost masters of this mind-set is Jim Johnson, the longtime defensive coordinator of the Eagles (who in spring 2009 took a leave of absence to battle cancer). What Johnson's

Eagles have done as well as anyone is vary their pressures and blitzing schemes to keep opponents off-balance. "I felt years ago that the name of the game is getting to the quarterback, causing turnovers, and creating negative plays," Johnson says. "That's when you win games. I don't think you can sit back. You have to be aggressive. Sometimes I'll blitz on the first play of a game to get after them and set a tone with my players. For a while there the offenses were putting pressure on us with a lot of different formations and with situational substitutions. My thing is to try and put pressure on them. I want to make them start thinking."

Johnson has perfected a style of play that puts a great deal of pressure on identifying the primary rushers. Most offenses in today's game focus their line calls on the position of the Mike (the middle linebacker; the terminology has evolved from the legendary coach Clark Shaughnessy's mnemonic cues, and today the middle linebacker is Mike, the weak-side linebacker is Will, and the strong-side linebacker is Sam). Johnson is constantly changing the look of his defenses in hopes of disrupting the "count" of the offensive line and backs as to who blocks whom. "We will change up our looks from one week to the next. If we can get them to just hesitate, pause, with regards to their assignments, we can create an opportunity for our rushers to win. It is all about isolating the best matchups with the best angles we can get."

Johnson, like many coordinators, has a very specific idea of what kind of player he wants, and like Bill Belichick in New England, he puts a great deal of emphasis on football intelligence. "We all want speed, but I like guys with football smarts," he says. "I want players who can think. They don't have to be off the charts on tests, but I like someone who can read the situation and react to it."

It was one of Johnson's protégés, former Giants' defensive coordinator Steve Spagnuolo, now head coach of the St. Louis Rams, who orchestrated the Super Bowl march of the New York Giants in the 2007 season, culminating in an epic Super Bowl XLII performance in which they sacked Tom Brady five times.

One common theme in many modern defenses is the emergence of "hybrid" players, who can play both a defensive end and a linebacker position. The virtues of this kind of fast, often undersized player is significant. If he is credible in run defense, he can be a nightmare for offensive coordinators to plan for.

Much of an offense's planning depends on knowing the roles of the defenders it's facing. But the best hybrid players, like Dallas's DeMarcus Ware, San Diego's Shawne Merriman, and Baltimore's Terrell Suggs, can confound an offense, because it doesn't know what the player will do. He may line up as a rush end and drop into coverage, or line up in a position in which a player would customarily have pass coverage responsibilities, then burst through a gap in the line on a pass rush.

Rex Ryan, the son of the famed Buddy Ryan and current head coach of the Jets, has proven to be one of the most inventive at developing and moving these hybrid players around. With Adalius Thomas, now with the Patriots, Rex had the consummate hybrid player. Thomas played five different positions with the Ravens in 2005. Thomas's use as a secondary player resulted from our being tapped out at the safety position by injuries in that same year. You can imagine the look on my face when Rex came into my office and suggested we use Adalius, all six-five, 285 pounds of him, in the secondary.

Hybrids aside, the aggressive, attacking defenses usually put an emphasis on fast corners, although the modern "shutdown" corners, with blinding speed and good technique, are expensive and hard to find. "I don't like fast corners," says one longtime

NFL defensive coach. "Because when fast corners make a mistake, they get *way* out of position."

In 2001, I wanted to get the talented Mike Nolan on my staff. He'd spent his whole career on the defensive side of the ball, but when he was let go from the New York Jets, the only position I had on my staff was as a wide receivers coach. I literally jolted up in my bed one evening, with the epiphany, "What if I brought this accomplished defensive guy to sit in on every offensive meeting, and bring his perspective to the discussion?" Most teams will have their staff members provide a self-scout of the opposite side of the ball, but that is a limited exercise. The idea of someone of Mike's credentials actually participating daily with the formation of an offense was intriguing. And it worked well. There was many a time when we as offensive coaches would question whether we should try something, and almost talk ourselves out of what looked like a good idea because of our conjecture about how the defense would adjust to it. Then Mike might say, "You are giving them *way* too much credit over there, in their ability to adjust to that." Mike has spoken many times about the value he placed on spending just that one year on the offensive side. He became my defensive coordinator the next year, after Marvin Lewis left to become the head coach of the Bengals.

Everybody's going to make mistakes in the days of multiple personnel sets and exotic defensive coverages. What you have to hope is that the big plays outweigh the mistakes and that your defense can set the tone of the game. If not, there's a feeling of powerlessness that can pervade an entire organization. There's nothing worse in football than being subjected to one long drive after another, and feeling as if you just can't get your defense off the field.

On the other hand, when you assemble a stout, formidable

defense, it will be more reliable than an equally skilled offense. It will experience fewer fluctuations from one week to the next. It will be less susceptible to weather or venue. It will, in short, keep you in most games. It will let you go on the road and defeat quality opposition. Over the ebbs and flows of a sixteen-game season, a quality defense is the surest way there is to get you to January.

And getting to the playoffs in January is what lets everyone keep their jobs.

WORKING ON A DREAM

When the Ravens won the Super Bowl in 2001 in Tampa, I stayed up all night celebrating with family and friends. On the plane back to Baltimore the next morning, I felt a powerful sense of relief and satisfaction. More than one person told me, "Enjoy it, because even if you're as good as you think you are, it won't happen that often." I was mindful of appreciating the moment that so many smart coaches and brilliant football players never experience.

But I also took some time with Ozzie Newsome to go over the Ravens' roster and contract situations for the off-season ahead. We had difficult decisions to make on both sides of the ball. Less than twenty-four hours after we lifted the Lombardi Trophy, we had begun thinking about—and working on—the next season.

When does the season start? Some coaches will look you in the eye and tell you the new season starts the morning after the previous season ends, and in the sense of planning and preparation, it does. Others tag the new season as the first day of training camp, in late July.

Of course, teams are working more or less constantly in those intervening months: coaches on evaluating the roster and preparing for April's draft, players on staying in shape, beginning with a sixteen-week postseason lifting cycle, and general managers on negotiating with free agents and draft choices. But much of that activity is transitional, the getting from the end of one period to the beginning of the next.

One key moment in this process is the day when the next season's schedule is released, in mid-April, a couple of weeks before the draft. It's hot-stove time for football. Most of the big free agents are signed, speculation is swirling about each team's wants and needs, and draft frenzy is starting to peak. It's nearly three months since anyone has played and another three months until anyone will play again.

And then the schedule comes. For decades, NFL executive Val Pinchbeck handled the schedule, before graduating to an advisory role for Dennis Lewin in 1998. Since 2005, former ESPN and ABC executive Howard Katz, the chief operating officer of NFL Films, has overseen the complex matrix of variables required to put the schedule in place. Everyone wants to start at home, end at home, and not have any three-game road trips, so almost everyone is sore when the schedule comes out. It is the rare team indeed that doesn't look at its own schedule and decide the league "is out to get us" because of some perceived slight. "When just about everyone is mad at me," says Katz, "I know I have done a good job."

In offices, coaching staffs crowd around the computer screen and study the fall itinerary. Just like fans, we take a long look, speculating on the rhythms of the upcoming season, what teams might be improved, which ones will be worse. Even though we know better than to think the record of a team from one year is any real indicator of its ability the next, we still fall into the trap. Just like fans, we mentally note what the playing schedule is going to do to our Thanksgiving and Christmas holiday planning.

Coaches are always preparing, breaking down film from the

previous season, evaluating possible free agents, revamping playbooks. But much of this thinking is theoretical. With the new schedule, players and coaches have evidence of the objective challenge that's facing them.

The opponents themselves, which have been known since the end of the previous season, are determined by a rotation system (each division cycles every three years through the other divisions in its own conference and every four years through the divisions in the other conferences), with two additional opponents determined by position scheduling—by where you finish the previous season. But the sequence of those opponents can make all the difference. Whether it's opening on the road against the defending world champions or facing two trips to the West Coast, or playing three playoff teams in succession right before a bye week, the schedule always offers its own challenges.

Everyone says they take the games one at a time. They don't.

The collective-bargaining agreement limits the number of times you can bring players in to practice in the off-season, but sometime in late May and early June, teams will hold their Organized Team Activities, better known as OTAs, and mini-camp. OTAs are the NFL version of the longtime high school and college practice of spring football. It is a term that was created in the legal jargon of the NFL's collective-bargaining agreement to define a strict code covering who can practice, what types of drills can be run, voluntary/mandatory attendance, and the amount of contact in OTAs.

Anecdotal evidence suggests that many coaches try to skirt these regulations, an issue that will surely come up in the next collective-bargaining negotiation. As a coach, you can become very creative about the ambiguity of terms like "noncontact," "reasonable meeting time," and "non-football-related drills." I once worked at a college where we stretched the definition of "non-football-related drills" in some spring workouts. One day a faculty member, whose parking spot was next to our practice field, complained to the athletic director about our illegal workouts. The next day, when the professor came to the university, he found that his parking spot had been moved to the other side of campus. If only it were that easy. Today the players, their union, and the ever-vigilant eye of the media make it next to impossible to skirt the CBA and the amount of time you are allowed with the players in the off-season.

Other than the designated veteran minicamps (maximum of three days), all workouts are voluntary, though "voluntary" is in this case a relative term. In the early seventies, when Bill Walton was playing for coaching legend John Wooden at UCLA, Walton objected to Wooden's instructing his players to keep their hair short. "Bill, there is no team rule preventing you from wearing your hair long," Wooden told him. "But I will tell you, I decide who plays and who doesn't, and I like short hair." In the NFL, head coaches like their players to show up for the voluntary OTAs.

Everyone conducts their OTAs a little differently. Some prefer to group them together to accommodate the players' schedules in hopes that they will all attend. Others will string out the workouts over a maximum number of days in hopes that players will be around the facility a longer time and get other things done "on their own" (if the quarterback wants to work on some routes with his receivers, if linemen want to stay a few more days and do some more weight training, that's all to the good). From a risk-management viewpoint, players working out, even informally, at the team complex are less likely to get in trouble than players on their own back home. One of the things the players surely will address in the new collective-bargaining negotiation in 2009 is consolidating and shortening the period of time teams can run their OTAs. Oddly enough, using the old original college guidelines of having thirty days to get in twenty practices might be the answer.

Regardless of how a team runs its "spring" sessions, it will be the first time a coach can see his entire new roster all together. Holdover players, rookies, and free-agent signings will all dress out and offer the coaching staff some sense of how those pieces cohere. At times, the staff will discount what it sees. When we brought Dawan Landry into camp in 2005, as a fifth-round draft choice, we knew we desperately needed a safety to partner with Ed Reed. Landry looked like a veteran in the OTAs, but none of the coaching staff wanted to go out on a limb and hail him as the starter. Three days into real training camp, after we'd seen him in pads, we knew: He was the real deal.

But too often, we err in the other direction. Coaches get excited over someone who can do all the right things in shorts but who, when the action starts and he's being hit and in pain and trying to make snap decisions, won't be able to perform at a starter's level.

The real objective of OTAs is twofold. First, it gives players a starting point for their off-season workouts. There are three kinds of conditioning for a football player: You can get into shape, you can get into football shape, and then you can get into hitting shape. Both the rules and the time of year prohibit you from working on the last of the three, but you can set the foundation for the first two. Football shape puts a player through the limitless cuts, explosions, and bursts that are part of this game. If a coach can set the foundation in late May and early June, players can build on that as they work toward the reporting date in late July.

The secondary objectives of OTAs and minicamps are to get a sense of where your focus needs to be in training camp and set a tempo for the way you expect your players to work. Because of the physical demands the long NFL season puts on the players, virtually every team has to stage most practices—particularly late in the season—with no pads. A player's first instinct when you take the pads off is to think it is an easier practice. You have to change that thinking and use the OTAs to show the players what you expect during the season.

Then comes the true off-season, all four weeks of it. For most people in the NFL, everything pretty much shuts down in late June. It's the calm before the six-month storm. It's when football families take their vacations. Most kids will tell you their summer is over when school starts. If you ask the sons or daughters of an NFL football coach when summer is over they will tell you at the end of July; that is when their dads go back to work 24/7. Those vacations before training camp are valuable and precious, and I wish I could say that I was self-actualized enough to live entirely in the moment during them. But as my wife and daughters can attest, even on a lake in Minnesota, my mind can drift to nine-on-seven drills that are still a month away. We would usually spend the last month of our limited vacation in the north woods of Minnesota on Lake Vermilion. Many a morning I sat on the dock watching the sun come up with a cup of coffee, making notes on the themes and lectures I would pepper the team with during training camp.

There are two dominant trends in training camps: First, they're getting shorter and shorter (most last just three or four weeks). In the seventies, training camps routinely lasted six weeks or more, and players dreaded that time, because it meant that they would be isolated from their families and spend much of their days in more or less constant physical anguish. (Remember that this was before being "in shape" was a year-round expectation.) The repeated battering from two-a-day workouts administered by coaches who were convinced that the only way teams could get tough was by beating the hell out of each other left players physically punished and emotionally spent.

A couple things have changed that. For starters, most players stay in shape year-round, so the need for a training camp environment that resembles the Bataan Death March is reduced. When I was on the staff of the 49ers, Bill Walsh did a study and found that the time of the year in which players were *most* fatigued was after training camp, before the first game of the season. This led him to scale back extensively on the amount of hitting his teams did in training camp, one of the more influential innovations he brought to the game. I can remember him saying more than once about his team, "Our number-one priority is to get them to the opener as healthy and as fresh as possible."

The other trend is less welcome in some circles. Increasingly, teams don't get away to sleepy college towns for training camp, instead holding it at their home facility or very close by. The old-school method of going hours away from home, to some small, isolated college, has its merits. There is a Spartan atmosphere that's all about football, and that encourages bonding and camaraderie. Fans show up by the tens of thousands, and that's a valuable time in which players interact most directly with the people who make their lifestyle possible.

On the other hand, there's no question that having training camp close to home is more economical and more efficient. People sleep better in their own beds. In Baltimore, when we had training camp out at Westminster College, I gave the veteran players the option of sleeping at home. This custom has become more and more accepted around the league with those teams that are close enough to do so. At first even the players looked at this skeptically. The conventional thinking was that the player needed the additional structure, and that coming and going to meetings and practice would be chaos. In nine years as the head coach of the Ravens I always had a curfew, but never a "bed check." My thought was always that if I had to go and knock on the door of a grown man to see if he was where he was supposed to be, doing what he was supposed to be doing, we had greater problems than whether that particular player was out late or not. This was part of developing a sense of accountability to your profession and your team. In nine years with the Ravens we never had a problem related to the players' being allowed to go home in the evenings. I made it clear that if we did have any problems with players being late or missing meals, meetings, or workouts, I would yank them all back into the team hotel. As I told them, "Then you go tell Ray Lewis why he can't go home at night and sleep in his own bed."

If you sat a head coach down and strapped him to a poly-graph, he would admit that going into training camp, he prob-ably already knows forty-five to fifty of the guys who are going to make his regular-season roster. In that sense, training camp is about selecting the last five guys on the team. But then there are crucial questions about development, both for units and for individual players.

Everybody does something new on both sides of the ball every season. I have yet to hear an offensive or defensive coordi-nator stand up in front of his players on the first day of training camp and tell them, "Guys, same drill as last year. We're just going to have all the same plays and work on executing them better." Innovation is an integral part of the game. So there's a constant tension, throughout the preseason, over how much of your new offensive or defensive looks to show. You want to hone your team and get ready for the season. But you don't want to give your first opponents a free sneak preview of your new variations. The conundrum is keeping the players focused on schemes and tactics that don't get reinforced in any of the four preseason games you play.

Individually, players are under a terrific amount of pressure to do something to get the coaching staff's attention. I tell players in camp: "I'll cut you when I have to. But don't cut yourselves. Don't do something stupid that's going to prevent you from having a chance to make the team." Coaches learn to be tolerant of mistakes and able to see progress when it occurs. A coach has to be able to figure out, Is this guy not a player, or is he a player who is just not grasping it yet?

In the course of training camp and the four exhibition games, you also have to realize that the purpose is not to win football games now so much as to get ready to win football games during the season. So in preseason games, starters play a lot less than they used to. They may play fifteen snaps the first game, a quarter and a half of the second game, a half and a drive the third game (to condition them to making halftime adjustments and coming back out with the same sharpness and focus), and often not at all the final game. Typically you will try to get your starters about a game and a quarter (roughly a hundred snaps) going into the season. Their playing time is regulated and watched closely by the head coach, almost like a pitching coach watches a pitcher's pitch count in baseball.

Then the real thing starts, and a coach hopes that the past eight months of preparation has put the team in the position to excel during the seventeen weeks to follow. As soon as the last preseason game ends and the final cuts are made, we all go into regular-season mode. The hours are long, the focus is sharp, the attention span at the meetings is longer.

All over the league the week before the season, everyone's starting to guess. You always think you're going to be good, if you're worth a damn at all. You project, you think, *Surely we can win almost all of our home games . . . and then we can steal a game here and a game there on the road.* The rule of thumb is that to make the playoffs, you have to beat the teams you should beat, then split with the good ones.

In the real world you attempt the impossible, pointless task of trying to guess how many games you're going to win, and how strong your opponents are going to be. You say you don't do it. It's silly to do it. Everyone knows that the teams you wind up playing won't be what you think they'll be. But people do it anyway.

Then on some gorgeous hot September Sunday, nearly five months after the schedule was first published, the teams take the field. And each year, once I get to the regular-season opener, I am struck by the energy, the passion, the speed at which the game is played in the opener.

Kickoff Weekend is a good reminder of the zero-sum nature of professional football. Going in, everyone is sunny and optimistic. Everyone is convinced they're going to be better. But sixteen teams will come out of that first weekend at 0–1.

And when you lose that first game, it can be devastating. The difference between victory and defeat is magnified the next day. You walk into a team complex on the Monday after a victory and everyone is happy to see you. Receptionists are cheerful and bright and answer the phone on the first ring. The coffee tastes better. Your assistants, even if they didn't get much sleep, have smiles on their faces. Everyone in the building has a smile on his or her face.

After a loss, the collective mood is completely different. The lights don't seem to be as bright, there's a palpable gloom in the air, you feel more tired. Everyone goes about the day's tasks, but the defeat seeps through the walls.

You can intellectualize and say people shouldn't respond that way. But guess what? They do. A single loss mortifies the building. You spend longer the next day going over film, then you take longer walking your players through the previous day's mistakes. You don't get to start on the next opponent until 5:00 or 6:00 P.M. You are flat. Questions start—especially in today's media universe—and all losses are blown out of proportion. You can have one of the best teams in football, but if you open on the road against a better team, you're still winless. And people all over town are asking, *What's wrong with the team?*

Often, the answer is that nothing's wrong. But it's only a week into the season and someone has to lose each game. Some teams know they're good right away. And some teams discover they're bad right away. But for most teams, the work in progress takes longer to sort itself out. You'll get through the first quarter and sometimes the first half of the season not entirely sure whether you're going to be a contender or an also-ran.

There are times when crucial decisions have to be made. The season the Ravens won the Super Bowl, we started hot with Tony Banks as our quarterback. Early on, we rallied to beat a Jacksonville team that we hadn't defeated before, and that win gave the team a great deal of momentum. But through the end of September and early October, Tony was so inconsistent that his play was threatening the whole team. I knew then that we had a special defense, but the problem wasn't just that the offense couldn't win games for us, it was losing games for us.

Over the course of that season, I was able to make three key assessments that would prove crucial. First, it became obvious to me that we did indeed have a truly dominant defense, one that under the right circumstances could shut down any opponent we would face. Second, I observed that we had sufficient offensive assets (for example, outside speed to make just enough big plays) and a solid running game so that, given solid quarterback judgment that minimized turnovers, we could excel without a truly explosive offense. Last, I saw that there was not another team in the league that was playing at such a dominant level as to require us to abandon our formula for winning. Parity had truly arrived in the NFL, and we had the assets we needed to take advantage of that balance. Clearly, it was time to "think outside the box."

Collectively, these assessments meant that I had to fundamentally change the way I would orchestrate the game. Ball control, field position, and clock management became my primary focuses. During the course of the week when I might catch a game on television, either pro or college, I would normally be drawn to a formation or a sequence of plays a particular team might be using. Now, I found myself paying more attention to how other coaches were using their time-outs, or when they were electing to punt or go for it on fourth down.

As the media began to pick up on our change in approach, I began to sarcastically joke about being drawn into the "dark side" of the game, to provoke those who believed I was more interested in statistics than wins. Some failed to see the humor in it, or perhaps didn't want to acknowledge that I was willing to adapt. What they failed to recognize was that I was at least smart enough to grasp the simple truth: Coaches are evaluated purely on wins and losses.

As this transformation took place, it become apparent to me that Trent Dilfer was the man to take the helm. Tony had shown flashes of brilliance and possessed physical tools Trent would have loved to have. But Trent had the maturity and poise to recognize what we needed to do to win.

You hear the phrase all the time, and quarterbacks hate it, but Trent knew how to manage the game. Late in the season we were playing the San Diego Chargers with a chance to seal our ticket to the playoffs, the first in franchise history. Late in the game we were comfortably ahead, with the ball on the Chargers' twenty-yard line, and a time-out was called. As we discussed the different plays we might run I was throwing out option after option that would have Trent taking a shot into the end zone. Trent coolly said, "Coach, all we need to do is run the ball, kick the field goal, and we win. Why risk the other?" He was right. I was thinking more like a play caller than a head coach.

I've been in other seasons, in which injuries or lack of talent or some combination thereof make it impossible to win consistently. When the losses build, a collective inertia starts to take over, and you're just looking for a way out. And as coaches, we dread the day we have to face the team after we've been mathematically eliminated.

Pro athletes are a prideful group. You have sixteen games, and have to play at an emotional, passionate, committed level. It's not that players don't play hard when they're eliminated, but sometimes they don't play with total commitment. They're not even consciously holding anything back, just not giving themselves as fully as they do when the playoffs are at stake. (As the old Texas Tech coach Spike Dykes once put it, "Right now our team is like the ham-and-egg sandwich. The chicken is involved, but the pig is really committed." When you get to the end of a season where you're not going to the playoffs, almost everyone is still involved, but not enough people are committed.)

On the other hand, the alternative is equally hard to quantify but nonetheless real. When a team gets to December and is in the hunt—8–4, 7–5, in that area—you can tell. Practices are crisper. A team and its employees recognize that you are within striking distance of the playoffs. There's a clarity of purpose that you don't always have earlier in the season.

Players are staying after practice to look at film. No one's late for meetings. Even the locker room is cleaner. And, as a coach, you can let up a little bit. If the team looks sharp and focused, you might get through practice fifteen minutes early, and let your guys go.

But the single factor that most affects the course of the season for good or ill is the one no one can control: injuries. One of the reasons no one is right back in early September, when trying to evaluate how good they'll be and how good their opponents will be, is that no one can adequately predict what the injury situation will be like.

With a fifty-three-man roster and a salary cap, no team has the sort of depth it wants. That means that if a team gets really beat up, it's forced to improvise, moving players out of position or, alternatively, signing someone off the street, although many of the players you'll sign at that point have been tagged with the ultimate scout's dismissal—"He's just a guy."

As a coach, I try to be sensitive to the physical toll. Around the league, practices taper off as the season progresses. This is where the cumulative benefit of the OTAs should come in. Your team has to understand how to practice without pads, and without hitting. They have to be perceptual learners who are able to take something from the classroom right onto the practice field with minimal reps. In September, the sequence of Wednesday/Thursday/Friday practices might find the players dressing out in pads/pads/shells (the latter referring to all players wearing shoulder pads and shorts, with minimal contact). In October, you'll switch to shells/pads/shorts (this meaning no shoulder pads, and virtually no contact). By November it's shorts/pads/shorts, and by December it's just shells/shells/shorts.

Injuries are the wild card, the confoundingly uncontrollable factor that often influences a season one way or the other. A halfway decent team that stays healthy can find itself in contention for a division title. But even a good, veteran, deep team that gets banged up in critical areas can have a season short-circuited.

Sometimes the impact of an injury can be felt not just in the position itself but throughout an entire unit. When the Ravens lost defensive tackle Trevor Pryce in 2007, it affected not only our interior run defense but our pass rush as well. With Pryce in, teams had to use two players to account for his presence inside, freeing Terrell Suggs to frequently face single coverage on the outside. But with the falling dominoes after Pryce's injury, teams could man-block his replacement one on one, offering more opportunities to run and freeing personnel to add to the outside protection.

The same thing happened in 2007—a nightmare injury year if ever I saw one—with our cornerbacks. A team can stand the loss of one corner. You can roll your coverages to the side where your backup is playing. But lose two starters—as we did in losing Samari Rolle and Chris McAlister—and you're out of business. We couldn't play a standard seven-man front. We'd have no choice but to sit in a Cover 2 all day and get slowly sliced to pieces.

You also have to be sensitive to the human component. Coaches and players alike have to have tunnel vision. They can't prepare for the future by bemoaning the absence of their best players. So there's a tendency to respond the same way to any injury: *We'll just have to work harder; we'll miss Billy Bob but this young rookie is going to step up and play his best, and everyone else will just have to rally around him.*

In the real world, there can be a coldness to this. The same guy you said was an indispensable part of the team one day gets injured the next. You're concerned about his health and his morale, and you miss his presence. But you have to go on.

"Ain't no NFL team a family," Warren Sapp once explained. "That's the one word we use in this league that's the biggest lie ever. . . . 'Cause if we're a family and the baby's lagging behind we all stop and make sure that baby's safe. In a brotherhood of men, we go. You don't wanna come with us, you stay there. We go. That's what a football team does."

Warren exaggerates for effect, but to a large extent what he says is true. You have to adapt. You can't go through the season bemoaning the loss of your best players.

The year after the Ravens won the Super Bowl, we looked nearly as good on defense and even better on offense. But then Jamal Lewis went down with a torn anterior cruciate ligament in training camp, and when the medical report came back that he was going to be out for the season, we knew we were screwed. Lewis was the key to our power running attack, and we were thin at the position because we'd let Priest Holmes go in free agency.

When you lose a player of this magnitude, this early in the season, you literally get sick to your stomach. Your first instinct is to panic, howl at the moon, and cry in your beer. But you know you can't let the panic show. Mike Smith, head coach of the Atlanta Falcons, observed of his first year, "Not letting your emotions or overreactions show was the hardest thing I had to get used to. I never realized how much people in the organization and particularly the team picked up on my demeanor." So you calmly tell your team, the organization, the media, and the fans that everything will be okay and the next man will step up. Then you go home, yell at your wife, and kick the dog. But sometimes the staff adapts. In 2001, we were left with Jason Brookings at running back, so we brought Terry Allen out of retirement and eked out a 10–6 record and got to the divisional round of the playoffs.

If a good team avoids the injury bug and plays within itself, and gets a few bounces and kicks to go the right way, that team makes the playoffs. And everything that is good about football gets even better. Playoff football is special. It's not just that the stakes are higher. The games are better and more fiercely played. They stay in the memory well after most regular-season battles are largely forgotten. There's also a component of fear. When you get to the playoffs, you go through each day with the presumption that you're going to be hard at work until the first Sunday in February. But for each team, there's the unspoken fear that it's all about to end.

The players on every team that makes the playoffs convince themselves that they have become a team of destiny. Take a look at Philadelphia in 2008. They had a horrible midseason, Coach Andy Reid benched Donovan McNabb, they came back strong, then tripped up late against Washington. They went into the last week needing all kinds of help: They had to beat Dallas, but they also needed Chicago to lose, and they needed Tampa Bay to lose, at home, to the 4–11 Raiders. When all those things happened, and they blew out the Cowboys with the playoffs on the line, they began to feel like they were *meant* to be the Cinderella team. After beating the Vikings and then the Giants, they got to go to Arizona and they *had to* think it was their year. Of course, by then, they were playing another team that was equally convinced it was a team of destiny.

Oddly, the sense of destiny the Cardinals developed did not

start until they got into the playoffs. The Cardinals were the first team in the NFL to clinch a spot in the playoffs in 2008. Granted, it was by winning the worst division in football (the NFC West), but they did it the first week in December with a 34–10 whipping of the St. Louis Rams. They then proceeded to get humiliated at home by the Minnesota Vikings, 35–14, and destroyed, 47–7, in one of the most lopsided games of the year, by the New England Patriots.

Arizona's last game of the regular season was a meaningless game against the 4–11 Seattle Seahawks. The only thing talked about all week was that the game would be Mike Holmgren's last as the Seahawks' head coach. I was doing the game for Fox and it was amazing for me to see at halftime the Cardinals were playing so poorly they were booed off the field by their fans, and deservedly so. They were able to regroup and beat the Seahawks 43–21 to finish the season at 9–7. Ken Whisenhunt has to be given great credit for holding on to what had to be a team with fractured confidence.

Whisenhunt made two critical decisions in the 2008 season. First, he benched the team's future franchise quarterback, Matt Leinart, in favor of the veteran Kurt Warner. The Cardinals had made Leinart the tenth overall pick in the 2006 draft, giving him a $50 million contract. He was the future of the team, but Whisenhunt announced at the time, "The experience of Kurt Warner is what this team needs right now." During the season, with the team's running game in shambles, he benched big-money free-agent signing Edgerrin James in favor of rookie Tim Hightower, who gave the team a crucial boost. When he lost effectiveness near the end of the season, James moved back into the starting lineup and was a major catalyst in the team's playoff run.

The 2008 NFC Championship Game, the Eagles at the Cardinals, was a good example of what the modern game of football is about. The single most interesting part of the game for me right now is its emotional ebb and flow. Good teams go on runs the way basketball teams do. And in football, with two good teams playing, the runs can be all the more dramatic, both because of what's at stake and because of the quality of the teams competing.

In the NFC Championship Game, the Cardinals jumped all over Philadelphia early, and took a seventeen-point lead. But then McNabb and the resilient Eagles fought back and tied the game at twenty-four, and suddenly they had all the momentum. But as we've seen happen before, the trailing team expended a terrific amount of energy in coming back (think of the Titans' rally from 16–0 down to the Rams in Super Bowl XXXIV, only to have the Rams, seemingly out of momentum, answer right back with an eighty-yard touchdown pass from Kurt Warner to Isaac Bruce). It happened again in the NFC title game. With the game knotted at twenty-four, and the game on the line, Warner directed the Cardinals on a touchdown drive to wrest both the momentum and the game back from Philadelphia.

All of a coach's decisions are magnified in the playoffs. Everyone questions playing a prevent defense with the lead, but the alternative is horrifying. If you get into a man-to-man or blitz situation and give up an eighty-yard touchdown pass that costs you the game and the season, you will get your ass barbecued. No one congratulates you for being brave enough to avoid playing the prevent defense.

When I was the offensive coordinator for the Vikings, we played a playoff game in New York with Randall Cunningham at quarterback. We were trying to rally late and yet we couldn't play a no-huddle. My quarterback wasn't able to call the plays at the line of scrimmage (he was much better when he could focus on executing the plays, rather than calling them), we had a third-string center who certainly wasn't going to be able to communicate the line adjustments if he had to, and we were playing in the Meadowlands, which meant none of our players could hear those calls anyway.

We got lucky, and won. But when I watched the taped broadcast later, I was getting my ass handed to me by commentator Joe Theismann, who was wondering why we weren't playing a no-huddle offense. The truth was, we couldn't. But there's no time to explain that during the game, and often no point in trying to explain it after.

When a team wins in the playoffs the players carry even more confidence into the next round. But when you lose it feels like death.

The worst loss I ever suffered was the one in the 2006 playoffs. We'd gone 13–3 with Steve McNair at quarterback. We had the Indianapolis Colts coming in for the divisional playoff round.

The city was filled with anticipation. Two wins and we were back to the Super Bowl, and we felt we could get there. The game was like an extended torment. We got inside the Colts' red zone five different times, but we could not punch it through for a touchdown.

Our defense had held the eventual Super Bowl champs to five field goals. We were inside the ten-yard line with a chance to take the lead when we threw an inexplicable interception. I say inexplicable because many times interceptions are just that. We had practiced the play countless times and were as confident in its execution as we were with any in the playbook. For some reason Steve McNair came off his primary target and tried dropping the ball off to Todd Heap, the last man in his progression of receivers. This is in no way blaming what happened on Steve. He had made countless throws in similar circumstances that were successful, and that was a major reason we were 13–3 and in the position we were. This time, however, an Indianapolis linebacker stepped in front of the pass and our dream was over.

There's nothing to be said at that point. The player can't hear the feedback, and there is always something on the field that the coach can't know or didn't see. You save it, perhaps bring it up later.

Of all the losses you can suffer, that first home game in the divisional round, when you've worked so hard to earn the bye, is perhaps the most painful. You work all season long and string so many good things together all to earn the reward of home-field advantage. And then you squander it in the first game. The whole season suddenly feels like a cruel joke.

I remember being so stunned and saddened that words failed me. "There's nothing I can tell you to make this any easier," I said to my team.

A loss like that lingers and lingers. It takes something out of you that you can't get back. And you go to sleep and you think of it, and you wake up, with crucial scenes from the game still in your head. And sooner or later, you realize you have to let it go. You have to because you can't change what happened, and guess what? The new season has started.

WINNING IS
EVERYTHING

Three days before Super Bowl XLIII in Tampa in 2009, the National Football League Players Association held a press conference and released a study by two University of Chicago economists who estimated that franchise values of NFL teams had gone up significantly in the past decade, and that owners were making an average profit of $25 million a year per team. A day later, at his annual "State of the League" press conference, Roger Goodell called the report "fiction."

The conflicting versions of reality looked like the sort of posturing you would expect between labor and management of a successful sports league with a new collective-bargaining negotiation just around the corner. But there was a great deal going on behind the scenes that revealed just how perilous the coming negotiations might be.

The Players Association itself was in the throes of its highly contentious, highly politicized eight-month search for a new executive director, which would end in March 2009 with the election of DeMaurice Smith, the shrewd Washington, D.C., lawyer who emerged as a viable compromise candidate. But the main focus of the press conference before the Super Bowl was to speculate on the owners' profits and sharpen the rhetoric about what the players were prepared for in the collective-bargaining negotiation that lay ahead. Then came the talk of the report, copies of which were released to the media at the end of the press conference.

The numbers will remain in question until the owners open their books, which they won't do. But the more telling fallout was in the note of disbelief seen later in the day by the league's representatives, who felt ambushed by the NFLPA. When Upshaw and Tagliabue were the key players in the framework of negotiations, there was a clear if unwritten understanding: *We're all in this together—no surprises.*

In the past, even if the Players Association was going to engage in such strident rhetoric, someone would have informed the management council that the public blast was coming and shared the economists' report in advance. Conversely, if the commissioner was going to hand down a suspension, he'd make a courtesy call to the executive director of the NFLPA first.

"Here's how Gene was," said one longtime insider. "If you were going to do something that would upset him, on a scale of one to ten, to a degree of four, he would be far more upset over that if it was a surprise than he would if you told him beforehand that you were about to commit a nine."

One of the reasons that the collective-bargaining agreement initially signed in 1993 has been renewed four times since then is that trust and spirit of communication built up between the players and management over the past fifteen years.

No more. Tagliabue's retirement in 2006 signaled a changing environment, and Upshaw's sudden and premature death in August 2008 meant that both sides would be led by relative newcomers in one of the most critical negotiations in league history.

The succession struggle for a new executive director was

unusually bitter, with the longtime executive staff backing former NFLPA president Trace Armstrong, while onetime NFLPA president Troy Vincent allegedly tried to unseat Upshaw before he passed away. (Smith's ultimate election in 2009 was probably good news for football fans. The election of either Armstrong or Vincent might have divided the Players Association and made the upcoming negotiations all the more difficult.)

Meanwhile, the NFLPA was facing a continuing crisis in its relationship with retired players. Upshaw had been brutally criticized by some retired players for the NFLPA's alleged lack of interest in the plight of NFLPA alumni. In December 2008, a federal court ordered the NFLPA to pay $28.1 million to retired players for cutting them out of marketing deals like Electronic Arts' Madden video game, which paid $35 million to active players but none to retired players, even though the game included 143 classic teams of the past, filled with players whose jersey numbers, positions, and characteristics closely matched those of the retired players.

The biggest problem the former players have with the union (and the league) involves health benefits. They feel cheated and victimized by an NFL pension plan that pales—in both actual dollars and health coverage—in comparison to similar plans in the NBA and Major League Baseball for players of their generation. The lack of a substantial health benefits plan for pre-1977 players is what former Oakland Raiders great Howie Long called "the deep, dark secret nobody wants to talk about."

The league and the union will point to a number of programs that have been instituted in the past couple of years as being proof of improved treatment. An example was the formation of the 88 Plan, a joint effort between the league and the NFL Players Association named after John Mackey's jersey number. The Hall of Fame tight end for the Baltimore Colts in the late 1960s and early 1970s is probably the most notable victim of dementia among former football players. Under the plan, families of former players who have various forms of dementia can receive money for their care and treatment—up to $88,000 a year if the player must live in an outside facility, and up to $50,000 a year if the player is cared for at home.

One of the few blemishes on Upshaw's record as the NFLPA's executive director was the barrage of criticism he received from many retired players, who charged that Upshaw and the union had turned their backs on the men who helped build the game.

The facts show a somewhat different picture. Upshaw's primary focus, somewhat understandably, was on active players. When he took over the NFLPA in June 1983, it was coming off a failed fifty-seven-day strike the previous season and was more than $4 million in debt. Today, the union has more than $220 million in cash and assets. The average player salary has risen from $120,000 to $1.6 million under his watch. According to the NFLPA, the players' retirement plan has grown exponentially and now has assets of about $1 billion.

Upshaw was never shy about shooting back at his critics. "The guys that are criticizing didn't help build this organization," he once said. "They didn't help fight for these benefits that the players have, and didn't help fight for the improvements that are there. If you look back at the struggle and the fight, you don't see those guys. When I think back to the seventies when [the NFLPA] was starting, what we did and what we fought for, we couldn't get the support. We couldn't get the support to fight for pensions. When we went to court in '74, I saw guys cross the picket line when I was standing on it."

It's true that the NFLPA's benefits package for retired players lags behind that of the Major League Baseball Players Association, but you have to remember how far behind the MLBPA the NFLPA started. The NFL and the Players Association have been increasing benefits for disabled players year after year and collective-bargaining agreement after collective-bargaining agreement. There was an enormous jump in benefits in the union contract of 1993, after Upshaw led the players through a series of triumphant antitrust lawsuits that resulted in free agency and many other benefits.

Not all former players have been critical of the union's efforts. As former Raiders' lineman Tom Keating observed, "What other business increases pensions payments *after* the employee is on a pension? I am grateful to Gene Upshaw for the increases he has produced."

The apathy during the creation of the union that Upshaw referred to still exists to a greater extent with today's players. Longtime Vikings' All-Pro center Matt Birk, who signed with Baltimore in 2009, was shocked to see his current peers' lack of interest in programs like Gridiron Greats, which focuses solely on the plight of the physical and emotional difficulties of former players. Taking a leading role in the Gridiron Greats program in 2008, Birk donated fifty thousand dollars and also sent a letter to every NFL player encouraging them to donate a portion of their December 21 game check. Of the nearly seventeen hundred active players in the league, only about twenty—not 20 percent, but twenty total—donated to the cause.

Part of the difficulty is separating the legitimate needs and rights of former players from the demands of those who are simply trying to cash in on the financial success of the league and the union. Pro Bowl quarterback Drew Brees verbalized the sentiments of many current players when he said, "There's some guys out there that have made bad business decisions. They took their pensions early because they never went out and got a job. They've had a couple divorces and they're making payments to this place and that place. And that's why they don't have money. And they're coming to us to basically say, 'Please make up for my bad judgment.' In that case, that's not our fault as players."

Brees is right about some of his predecessors, but it's also true that the broken bodies of retired players—there's a certain slow, mincing, hunched walk that distinguishes many of the most battered veterans—are a reminder of how physically demanding the sport is. There's also the *emotional* part of retirement. Whether he is age thirty, thirty-five, or forty, there's very little to prepare a professional football player, especially a successful one, for the deflating experience of the end of a playing career. You can open a restaurant, you can redouble your charity work, you can throw yourself into business, but nothing will replace the urgency, camaraderie, and commitment of being a trusted part of a football team. Steve McNair was the consummate team player, and the quintessential warrior on the field. But months before his horrible death, I had heard he was foundering in his new life, having trouble adjusting to the often mundane realities of a world without football. Between the numerous physical ailments and the often wrenching emotional adjustment, it's a difficult chapter in a lot of lives. Both the NFL and the NFLPA need to do a better job at providing support for players after their playing careers are over. This game will always be a tough way to get rich.

When the NFLPA finally elected a new leader in March 2009, there was a circling-the-wagons mentality that pervaded the association. Though the union had originally appealed the decision in the Electronic Arts case, Smith wisely pushed for a settlement with the retired players for nearly the full award, and preached unanimity—"I represent *all* the players," he said—among active and retired players. Smith was as eager as the owners to present a unified front in the negotiations, and mindful that his membership was determined to hold firm, resolute in not giving back any of the NFLPA's hard-earned gains.

Present rhetoric aside, the fact remains that for the most part, the National Football League has been a big, boisterous, mostly happy family. And why wouldn't it be? The NFL is rich, its product is in demand, and its primacy is at present unrivaled. The league is, according to *Forbes*, "the strongest sport in the world." Around the world, there are only four soccer teams—England's Manchester United, Liverpool, and Arsenal, and Spain's Real Madrid—valued at $1 billion. The NFL reportedly has nineteen teams worth that much, compared with none five years ago.

The teams appreciate in value even when they lose. The Redskins have had just three winning seasons in the decade since Daniel Snyder bought the team for $750 million, but since then the value of the franchise has increased to $1.5 billion, and in 2008 the Redskins played their home games to 110 percent capacity. Even the Detroit Lions, during their historically futile 0–16 season, still filled their stadium to 84 percent capacity, a figure that only ten Major League Baseball teams topped in 2008.

But there is a constant, inevitable tension between the players and the owners, between the league and its clubs, between the big-market teams and the small-market teams, between the "new guard" owners and "old guard" owners, and between the active players and the retired players. All of those tensions are heating up to a boiling point at the same time.

The NFL has been so successful for so long that there's a perception that the job of running the league is easy, or that, in the words of one sports blog, "a gorilla with a sixteen-pack box of Crayons could run the NFL and still make money at it."

In fact, the job is one of the toughest in sports, for all the reasons I've discussed: The commissioner must ride herd on thirty-two confident, voluble, powerful owners. He is elected by the owners. He is paid by the owners. He is their boss, but they are his as well. The tension between the league office and the thirty-two clubs is largely about autonomy. But the commissioner's job requires him to do more than keep the owners happy. It requires him to lead them while also balancing the needs of the seventeen hundred players and tens of millions of fans, as well as remaining vigilant about the league's reputation, the broadcast networks, and other corporate partners. Oh, and the one thousand employees who work under him.

The commissioner and his staff at 280 Park Avenue form the nerve center of pro football. It's not just the home office and corporate headquarters, but also the place where pro football starts, the White House to a nation of football constituents.

In most franchise businesses, I would guess that the home office thinks the satellite franchises are reckless and need direction, while the franchises think the home office is out of touch and needlessly haughty. But when the home office is the epicenter of the most valuable sports property in the world, and when the satellite franchises are worth nearly $1 billion each— and their annual dues to fund the league office are more than $5 million per club—that tension grows more pronounced.

The tension was less palpable a generation ago, when the league essentially negotiated all the lucrative sponsorship deals that the NFL signed. But when Jerry Jones called an end-around with his Texas Stadium sponsorship deal with Pepsi in 1995 (ten years, $40 million), in defiance of the league-wide sponsorship deal with Coke, it signaled a seismic shift in league-club relations. Many owners initially criticized him, but the majority eventually realized that Jones's more aggressive marketing stance could work for them, too. I was in Minnesota at the time and I remember thinking that other than the wearyingly familiar battles between Al Davis and the league office, this was the first time there was a breach in the "league-think" mantra among owners. The altercations with the Raiders became so continuous over so many issues that you never really thought of them as anything more than isolated cases specific to the Raiders. When Jones went "rogue" on the league it was the first eye-opening volley from ownership that said, "Hey, there may be a different way of doing this."

Suddenly, there were twice as many commercial opportunities in each area of sponsorship, though the leagues and clubs had to sort out where to draw the lines, so they didn't step on each other's deals. (This is still an issue. At Super Bowl XLIII, signage for MasterCard, a Raymond James Stadium sponsor, had to be replaced by signage for Visa, an NFL sponsor.)

New stadiums have been a key element in the growth in profitability of the league. And the league's G-3 stadium financing program, in which the NFL helped clubs finance their portion of the building costs from a central fund, was an example of how the league could play banker to encourage growth and provide financing that most clubs would not have been able to achieve on their own.

But more lucrative deals also meant higher player salaries and a need to continue increasing revenues, or "monetizing the game," as it's called within league circles. Newer stadiums meant more money, but also much greater debt loads than NFL teams were used to. The high-risk, high-reward environment the NFL has been living in looks a lot like the business world in which of many of the league's newest owners thrived. That's not a coincidence.

• • •

Meanwhile, Roger Goodell succeeded Paul Tagliabue as commissioner of the NFL on September 1, 2006. Even though Goodell had been in the NFL since 1982, his role was focused so much on the administrative side that we coaches had a very limited idea of what type of commissioner he would be. Upon taking office, Goodell immediately set about building relationships not only with the head coaches but with many others at the club level. Along with his top aides, he made a whirlwind tour of all the clubs. It was clear that he was building his working knowledge of the league, enhancing the many relationships he had developed over the years, showing everyone involved how interactive he wanted to make the commissioner's office, but still making sure everyone recognized he was "ready for prime time" and was now the man in charge.

Goodell dreamed about working at the league when he was growing up and has spent his entire adult life doing so. There hasn't been a commissioner better prepared for the job from the day he took over. But his daunting task wasn't made any easier by the fact that his three predecessors were all legends.

He lacked the done-everything, been-everywhere football knowledge of Bert Bell, who had been a player, coach, and owner before he became commissioner. Though he was used to dealing with the media, Goodell lacked the sophistication and reassuring presence of Pete Rozelle. And while he's smart, he didn't bring the towering intellect and steel-trap mind of Paul Tagliabue.

Yet Goodell has developed his own identity and demonstrated that he's got the character and gravitas for the job. There are striking differences in the perceptions of Tagliabue and Goodell within the league. Tagliabue came from a family of strivers, reared in a working-class environment in Jersey City, New Jersey. Goodell grew up the son of a U.S. senator, Charles

Goodell from New York. Yet it is Goodell who is viewed more as "one of us" by most of the executives in the league office and the clubs. "Paul knew just how to deal with the owners," said one longtime league executive, "but at times seemed dismissive of the rank and file of the league. Roger seems, at this early stage, to be able to relate more to the GMs, coaches, and administrative people."

Goodell rose through the business side, and because of that, saw and understood the coming storm well before most people outside the league did. He became a go-between for Tagliabue, who could be brusque and dismissive at times, and the rest of the owners, who are quite used to being treated with deference, thanks. He also worked through the endless hours of committee meetings that led to solutions that have made the league stronger, so he knows and has a good relationship with most of the owners—arguably closer than Tagliabue had.

Goodell also worked to bring more people with club experience to the league office. One of Goodell's top lieutenants is Ray Anderson, executive vice president/football operations. Anderson earned a BA degree in political science from Stanford and a JD degree from Harvard Law School. Anderson's experiences include being an agent for both players and coaches throughout the league. Besides myself, Ray has represented coaches Tony Dungy, Denny Green, and Herm Edwards. Anderson then went on to become vice president of the Atlanta Falcons before accepting a position with the league office.

I have known Ray Anderson for close to twenty-five years. He was my agent from my time as an assistant coach at Stanford University and brilliantly negotiated my first contract with the Ravens. His role included intervening with the league on my behalf for the many fines I accrued during my nine years with the Ravens. Between my criticism of officials and instant replay and my generally-just-stupid remarks, I have paid over seventy-five thousand dollars in fines. The late league administrator George Young (who had earlier worked as the Giants' GM) had my number on his speed dial. Like so many other coaches and NFL personnel, George had become a bit of a mentor for me, all the while taking my money in fines. After a long stretch of finally learning to keep my mouth shut, I asked him if he was finally comfortable in putting my file back in his cabinet.

"Let's just say I have put it at the bottom of the stack," cautioned George.

When my longtime friend and agent Ray took over George's job, I thought I was now home free, since Ray was the primary arbiter of fines. Regardless of the friendship, it was amazing to watch how quickly Ray started viewing matters from the perspective of the league. It did not take long before I had done something else to warrant a call from the league. But this time, the call came from my longtime friend.

"Brian, how are Kim and the girls doing?" Ray started the conversation. "Hope everything is well on the farm and you are doing well. When are we getting together to play tennis again?" Once I had settled comfortably into the conversational nature of the call, he lowered the boom. "Oh, by the way, I am fining you twenty-five thousand dollars for what you said last week about instant replay. I have already talked with your former agent [himself] and he doesn't think you have much of a case, so he advises you to just pay the fine." I figured it was futile arguing with two such accomplished lawyers.

Goodell's style is different from his predecessor's. The impression is that while Tagliabue would slowly build consensus, he was the sort who wouldn't be pushed: "If you need an answer now, the answer is no." By contrast, Goodell's staffers have learned that if they want to make any headway with him, they need to come with not just a report and options but a specific recommendation and a reason for it. Goodell is less tolerant of "blue-skying" a problem than his predecessor.

Though this attitude proves to be more in line with the "horizontal" model of business, with more emphasis on communicating and being more inclusive in the process, it is not without its pitfalls. During the Patriots' "Spygate" scandal in 2007, Goodell moved quickly to render judgment, to communicate clearly that the blatant violation of the rules wouldn't be tolerated. But in an age that increasingly values transparency in leadership, his decision to destroy the incriminating tape was more debatable—and bound to be viewed as burying the body by the media covering the scandal—and might have contributed to the story's playing out much longer than either the league or, certainly, the Patriots would have liked.

(One of the things I resented the most during that time was the assumption by some people that "all coaches do that." Well, no, we don't. I have coached for thirty years and have been in the NFL for eighteen years and never once have I seen or heard of anyone doing something so blatantly illegal.)

Tagliabue had more trouble swaying owners, so he chose to wear them down over time. The classic example of Tagliabue's leadership at its best came in 2001, when the league needed to realign, going from six divisions to eight divisions with the addition of the Houston Texans in 2002. There were myriad things to worry about, with every team angling for the best, most lucrative position.

But Tagliabue and the league office handled the process marvelously. In the realignment in 1970, teams had campaigned to be grouped in divisions with the other teams with the biggest, most modern stadiums, since teams got 40 percent of the net gate receipts from road games. As a way to circumvent that line of debate in 2002, the NFL decided that all visiting gate receipts would be pooled and split evenly, meaning that there would be no financial advantage to being in a specific division. Then came the long march of subcommittee meetings, many of which Goodell chaired.

What built over the course of more than a year was a growing consensus. With money off the table, teams could concentrate on tradition and natural geographical rivalries. The doctrine became: Last one in, first one out. Seattle, which had been an expansion team in 1976, made the jump to the NFC. Tampa Bay, in the black-and-blue division for only a quarter of a century, was lopped off to the newly formed NFC South.

In the end, realignment succeeded by removing the possible financial inequities from the equation. If the decision had been made purely for football reasons, the outcome would have looked precisely the same. This was league-think at its finest, and even those who were jockeying for something different capitulated in the end, allowing for the league to confirm the new alignment unanimously, which happens about as often for something substantial in the NFL as it does in the U.S. House of Representatives.

Commissioners tend to assert themselves more quickly than people suspect. Rozelle had moved the league offices from suburban Philadelphia to midtown Manhattan within five months of taking over in 1960, and he pushed through a joint television package within two years. Tagliabue, intent on eliminating the labor acrimony of the previous decade, had dinner with Players Association executive director Gene Upshaw within the first week of taking office in fall 1989, and they began working on the framework of a deal that would take four years to sign.

When Goodell arrived, he made it clear that in his mind, player behavior had become one of the main issues. Taking his case to the players directly, he suspended Adam "Pacman" Jones and Tank Johnson for a year, and put down harsh penalties for misbehavior. As he once explained it, "We need people to cheer for our players," which is a well-put summary of what the fan experience is about, as well as a lucid explanation of why player behavior is an important issue.

Goodell seems to understand that you have to be extremely clear and specific with the players in drawing a line when it come to player behavior. The message was delivered very early to the players: "Don't mess with this guy." Yet Goodell showed he could still be responsive to the owners when he bypassed the Competition Committee to allow Tank Johnson and Chris Henry to practice with their respective teams during their suspensions. This was a fundamental change in the rule that usually would not have been done until the off-season and a review by the Competition Committee and owners.

But make no mistake: Goodell got the job because he was seen as the candidate who was most likely to continue the NFL's soaring financial growth. And by the time he took over, the culture of the league was clear. No half measures. No accommodation. The NFL was the strongest brand in sports, and the owners made it clear that they wanted that brand exploited.

At the annual NFL meetings in March 2003, the NFL owners voted unanimously to form the NFL Network, a league-owned cable channel that would carry wall-to-wall football coverage, with heavy doses from the NFL Films vaults. The NFL Network was launched November 1, 2003, with plenty of promise and has been an artistic success, winning Emmy awards and critical praise.

From the NFL Network's inception, the league office made it clear that it wanted to give the network special access to create something extra and of added value. However, it also had to prove that it was not just a shill for the league and its teams. This balancing act has proven problematic at times. When the NFL Network was just getting started, Commissioner Tagliabue was asked by the coaches at the league meetings how they should deal with the network. His response was that the network had to establish its own credibility and therefore should be dealt with as just another of the "broadcast partners." Many were concerned that a media entity wouldn't be able to cover itself and retain credibility, but with the likes of reporters like Adam Schefter (who in 2009 was hired away by ESPN), the NFL Network has proven to be a viable outlet for all the league's news.

From the start, the league wanted to charge a premium price for the channel *and* have it offered in as many homes as possible, so it drove a very hard bargain in early negotiations with cable carriers like Comcast and Time Warner Cable. The big cable companies balked at the price and the terms, and questioned the value of the NFL Network, which at the time didn't have any live regular-season games to offer.

So skip ahead to 2004, when the league added an extra package to its arsenal of television offerings. It was a slate of mostly Thursday night games in the second half of the season, but the owners decided to pass on the best outside offer—Comcast's $450 million per year offer for the Thursday night package—

and bring it in-house, to the NFL Network. In doing so, the NFL Network increased its charges for cable carriers to about seventy cents per subscriber per month, in hopes of recouping the money. But the league has overplayed its hand, and has been unable to get distribution in enough homes (just 35 million in 2008) to make the sort of impact it desired, so in 2008 it made perhaps $100 million less in subscriber fees than it would have gotten from Comcast for the package.

Some industry experts say that the league should have sold the deal to Comcast or another cable carrier in 2003, then built the audience of the NFL Network slowly and steadily, initially picking up cable systems with a lower subscriber asking price (but one with an option to increase the per-subscriber charge if the network offered a slate of games). Then the network would have been dealing from a position of strength. People are much more likely to squawk over the possibility of losing something they already have than they are about not having something they want.

Beginning with a Thanksgiving night telecast in 2005, the NFL began expanding its Thursday night schedule, and now plays a schedule of seven straight weeks of Thursday night games, starting with Week 10. The games are on Thursday night because the NFL is prohibited by law from telecasting games on Friday and Saturday nights from September through November.

Nobody likes playing games on Thursdays. Players don't like it. Coaches hate it. As one league executive put it to me, "Football coaches want all games to begin Sunday at 1:00 P.M." It's true that we are creatures of habit.

But this is not just about coaches being rigid. You have to appreciate the condition players are in by the end of the season. For many, it's an effort to get out of bed on Monday, Tuesdays are spent mostly in intense rehabilitation procedures, and many players don't start feeling ready to play until Friday or Saturday. Playing two games in four days, at that time of year, is really harsh; the body heals only so fast. The NFL can take great pride in the way it has kept the health and well-being of the players as its top priority. Rule after rule has been implemented to protect the players from serious injury, and there is constant review of the way players use their bodies (particularly the head) in tackling and of ways to protect "exposed" players or players in a "vulnerable position."

Putting players, especially late in the season, at risk by shortening the week flies in the face of that mentality. But it's a compromise that is made in the name of "monetizing the game."

So the Thursday night series went to the NFL Network, where the league was counting on it to be an instant hit. Instead, these have been the least-watched national telecasts in pro football, because so few people could get the channel. Players and coaches grumbled about the timing of the games. Owners grumbled that the package wasn't more lucrative. The league seemed to be suing or being sued by every major cable carrier in the country. And fans grumbled for the obvious reason that they couldn't see the games they wanted to watch.

As I was watching this depressing drama play itself out, I couldn't help but think of my old boss Art Modell. Art used to go on at length about how the league was "going to kill the goose that laid the golden egg." Modell was a TV pioneer and, in his view, the league needed to treat the networks as the partners they truly were, being mindful not to gouge them for that last million, even if you could, so as to maintain a reservoir of goodwill.

To Goodell's immense credit, he eventually came to a similar realization. Beginning in November 2008, he began working quietly behind the scenes to repair the league's damaged relations with Comcast and the other big cable carriers. When Comcast and the NFL announced a settlement of their differences in May 2009, it opened the door for similar deals with the other large carriers.

In the short term, it meant that the NFL Network would receive less money than in the past (forty-two cents per cable subscriber per month in 2009, rather than the seventy cents the NFL Network had been charging), but the channel would now be carried on Comcast's main digital tier, paving the way for it to be in 10 million more homes by the beginning of the 2009 season. Eventually, it was expected that the other major carriers would sign similar deals, and the NFL Network would be much more accessible on the main digital tiers of the carriers across the country.

It was a terrific accomplishment by Goodell, who could sit down at the negotiating table with the NFLPA's De Smith in the summer of 2009 satisfied that he had broken the cable stalemate, and earned lucrative extensions with Fox and CBS on the network side, and DirecTV for the league's Sunday Ticket package. The NFL would enter the negotiations from a position of strength.

Though I admire much of what Roger Goodell has accomplished, I don't envy him his position. Even in light of the recent successes, he's still forced to contend with a group of determined owners on one side and a group of proud players on the other side, with both sides seemingly digging in for a long and potentially rancorous fight.

Meanwhile, the league's owners continue to push relentlessly for more and more revenue, entering into areas in which even some of the most progressive league business executives were uncomfortable. For more than fifty years, the league has had a firm opposition to gambling of all sorts. The NFL has dissuaded the networks from discussing betting lines, refused to even consider a franchise in Las Vegas, and opposed legalized football wagering from coast to coast. But in the spring 2009 meetings, the league announced it would allow teams to sell their logos to state lotteries. Within days, the Patriots and the Redskins had already struck deals ("My only surprise was that it didn't happen within hours," said one league executive), and other teams were working on them as well.

The perception is growing among league insiders that the league's priorities have changed. "Here's the difference," said one longtime executive and football lifer. "We used to start by deciding what was the best thing for the game, then try to figure out how to make the most money off of it. Nowadays the owners start by figuring out what's going to make the most money, then they try to figure out how to make it good for the game."

This environment was the backdrop against which the owners were taking an increasingly hard-line stance with the coming collective-bargaining negotiations. "You have to remember," one senior executive told me, "that the owners opted out of the agreement *before* the economy went down the drain. They were already displeased with it." The message seems clear: The owners are determined to get back a portion of what they think they lost in the 2006 CBA extension.

What gave that negotiation such a sense of urgency was the prospect of an uncapped year, and Gene Upshaw's vow that if the players ever rid themselves of a salary cap, they would never agree to restore it. Though the league was flush in 2006, the owners had a healthy fear of what an uncapped year would look like, in terms of both overall costs and how it would affect competitive balance. Their attitude is different this time. They're ready to call the players' bluff.

As for the players, I think it would be a mistake to underestimate them. They play a dangerous sport, and to succeed at it requires dedication. Off the field, they tend to be extremely motivated and extremely loyal. They can, given a compelling reason, be stubborn. One longtime NFLPA rep told me, "My biggest concern about this thing blowing up is that the owners are seriously underestimating our resolve to not go backward with regards to what we have already earned."

I asked a senior NFL executive to tell me his greatest fear about the coming negotiation, and he gave me a surprising answer. "I think the owners underestimate the players' ability to withstand an extended work stoppage."

The old-guard owners are wary of the new-guard owners. Both sets of owners are pressing the leadership to hold firm and come up with a more workable agreement. As one league executive put it, "This present deal is turning the moderate owners into Shiites." The players had been divided themselves, as the ugly succession struggle proved, but they seem unified behind their new leader and in the feeling that they're not going to give up their hard-won gains.

Neither side feels that it can give much ground. And I keep thinking of Ozzie Newsome's line about acrimonious negotiations: "You've got to give the agents their win."

There's wisdom in that.

And I wonder: Will the owners give the players their win? Will the players give the owner their win?

If the answer to both of those questions isn't yes, we may not have pro football in 2011.

GAME OF THE FUTURE

The rhetoric will grow increasingly harsh, the prospects for a quick resolution increasingly remote, and much of the fall of 2009 and the early months of 2010 will be filled with doomsday scenarios about what an uncapped year will mean to the game in the 2010 season. If no agreement is reached—and I don't think one will be in time—then the uncapped season of 2010 will be spent with even harsher rhetoric, and even more speculation about whether the salary cap can ever be recovered once it's gone, and whether the players and the NFL's management council will reach an agreement by the deadline, the last day in February 2011.

If they don't, then there's little doubt about what will happen next: The owners will lock the players out of team facilities on the first day of the 2011 league year, March 1, and the NFL will be facing its first work stoppage in twenty-four years.

As bad as that all sounds, I can promise you one thing: The reality, if it ever comes about, will be much, much worse.

Pete Rozelle often spoke about the benefit that sports gained by being both news and entertainment. But he was acutely aware of what happened when it seeped into the business or legal news. In the modern age, I think people have grown complacent about what an advantage the NFL has enjoyed because of extended labor peace. It's not just that the focus has largely been on the game on the field; it's that the game hasn't been paralyzed, in the way that every other major American team sport has been over the past fifteen years, by labor unrest.

Surely, you're thinking to yourself, the wiser minds will work this out, and football will remain together. Surely, the smartest sports league in the world won't suffer the same self-inflicted wounds that damaged Major League Baseball in 1994 and pro basketball in 1999 and hockey in 2005.

Surely the most successful sports league in the world, which generates $7 billion per year in revenue, and in which owners equally share in more than 80 percent of all revenue, will not die of self-inflicted wounds.

I hope not. Let me take a page from the coach's workbook and adopt a PMA—Positive Mental Attitude—and hope that it all gets worked out by 2010, and pro football remains in place as the most prosperous league in the world, with the sanest economic system in big-time professional sports.

What changes can we look forward to in that best-case scenario?

Start with the game itself, and its continued evolution and refinement.

Football is always moving. There are a hundred small examples like this: Go back and look at a picture of Jan Stenerud or Garo Yepremian, or almost any kicker from the seventies. You'll see the holder in each of those pictures with his back knee on the ground and his front knee flexed in a kneeling position. Now watch field-goal kickers today, like Adam Vinatieri or Neil Rackers, and you'll see that almost all of their holders take the opposite stance, with their front knee on the ground and their back leg up and flexed. Two things led to the change, which has evolved slowly through the ranks of pro and amateur football over the past forty years: First, the leg extended out front was more vulnerable to getting kicked, hit, or bruised. And whether the holder was a quarterback or a punter, that was usually a valuable leg. Second, holders found that having the back leg extended allowed for more accurate positioning on their placement in the event of off-target snaps. So a minor adjustment is made, repeated, imitated, and eventually adopted as the new industry standard.

Other aspects of the game are constantly evolving based on experimentation and the endless striving to find a competitive edge. There was once a day when wide receivers actually started each play in a three-point stance. So generations of defensive backs got to line up over a receiver who was in the worst possible position to accomplish his task, which was to burst out quickly and get free on a pass route.

As today's game continues to evolve, we'll see a continued increase in the use of no-huddle offenses, partly to combat the ever-growing complexities of defenses, and even more motions and shifts by the offense to give quarterbacks indicators about the types of coverage a defense is in. Defensively, teams will keep moving their safeties around, trying to find less obvious ways to build the popular "eight-man box" without overcommitting to stopping the run. Defensive coordinators will grow even more ingenious in disguising looks or creating mismatches with their hybrid pass rushers.

Of all these evolving areas, the two that might be the most noticeable, which are already being seen on a widespread basis in college football, are the twin developments of more shotgun formations and fewer huddles, due to offenses that make play calls at the line of scrimmage.

It's too early to pronounce the huddle on its last legs, but at the rate we're going, it could be on the endangered species list. And it's conceivable that, someday, technology will render the huddle obsolete anyway. In 1979, Bill Walsh's first year in San Francisco, starting quarterback Steve Deberg came down with laryngitis before our game in New Orleans. With the crowd noise in the Superdome there was no way Deberg was going to be able to call signals loudly enough for his teammates to hear. Being in the heart of Silicon Valley, the ever-innovative Walsh had Deberg outfitted with a small amplifying device with speakers implanted in his shoulder pads, so his calls were amplified.

Although this is now illegal, we may see the day when all offensive players are equipped with helmet transmitters to receive signals and plays from the quarterback, or even instructions from the sideline.

But at this point, the league still won't let the coach-to-quarterback communication come from the booth, just the sideline (where it's now relayed from the booth), and coaches are as yet not allowed to use anything other than Polaroids to show players what has occurred on the field. This could change; the league has been experimenting with digital screens that would allow coaches more freedom to use replay equipment on the field or in the locker room at halftime.

Though running a full-time offense with no huddle would add more plays, it would require even more specialization, and many football purists feel that the game is already too specialized. One of the game's great pluses on television is the natural interval in the action that the huddle provides, which is perfect for instant replay, and allows a better understanding on the part of fans about what just happened.

Elsewhere on the field, there seem to be a few absolutes about the future. With the research already done on concussions, the game will surely continue to grow safer, and it will have to, because one of the other certainties is that players will continue to grow bigger, stronger, and faster, meaning even with more stringent rules for safety, the collisions will be more forceful than before.

Goodell began his tenure as commissioner dealing with player actions as aggressively on the field as he has off. "We have to do whatever we can to remove any of the techniques that can unnecessarily risk injury to the players," he said. He warned the league would continue to aggressively penalize flagrant fouls, and said dangerous tactics were used less in the second half of the season after his enforcement early in 2008.

However, future changes in the rules will elicit plenty of player resistance. Players come up through the game with a clear understanding of what is and isn't clean play, and they resist having that definition changed for them by the league. "We understand what the league is trying to do, and we all want to stay safe," said Chris Harris, the Carolina Panthers' safety, "but frankly if you play the game thinking about all the things the league is fining right now you won't last very long."

Troy Polamalu was less diplomatic. "The game loses so much of its essence, and it really becomes like a pansy game," the Steelers' Pro Bowl strong safety said. "I think regarding the evolution of football, it's becoming more and more flag football, two-hand touch. We've really lost the essence of what real American football is about. I think it's probably all about money. They're not really concerned about safety."

As cynical as Polamalu's perspective might seem, there is logic to ownership's wanting to protect their most valuable assets. "When you think of all the time, energy, and resources we put into identifying, procuring, developing, and paying for the player it only makes sense to protect him," said one owner.

"The moral and ethical obligations aside, it just wouldn't be good business if we didn't." Some have charged that the league is only protecting its stars, but this is clearly false. One of the main rule changes at the annual meetings in 2009 was outlawing the three-man blocking wedge, a rule that provides extra protection for the most anonymous players in the game.

Within five years, we might have helmets equipped with computer chips that would instantly monitor where the major impact points might be and use small inflatable pads to combat the severity of shock.

The league is particularly sensitive to the safety issue now, when the issue of retired players' health benefits is such a flashpoint. Right now, a ten-year veteran who retires from the NFL has his health care covered for five years following the end of his career. Neither the NFL nor its teams can afford to provide full health-care coverage for players for the rest of their lives, but it does seem that the league and the Players Association—both acutely aware of health problems faced by retired players— might work harder to create some optional additional coverage options that would allow players to put, say, an additional $125,000 a year into a fund that would, after eight seasons, have $1 million plus interest in it, enough to guarantee retired players full health coverage for life. It doesn't matter that this is perceived as a union issue. Retired players who are crippled and destitute reflect on the league itself.

Off-field changes will be just as prevalent, and you can see them taking shape already.

In November 2008, I sat in the United Terminal at San Francisco International Airport waiting for the red-eye back to Baltimore after doing the Detroit Lions versus the San Francisco

49ers game for Fox. I had a couple of hours to kill so I stationed myself at one of the many cafés in the main rotunda that feeds to the multiple terminals at SFO.

I opened my MacBook Air and logged on to the NBC site to watch Sunday night's game with the Dallas Cowboys taking on the Green Bay Packers. NBC has a marvelous interface that allows you to watch the game from one of five different perspectives (end zone, sideline, isolations, and so forth). At the same time I had a document open making notes on the game I had just called for Fox. After a few minutes my wife Skyped in. (Skype is an online service that allows you to teleconference face-to-face for free; I always feel the need to explain what I mean when I say I am "Skyping" my wife, lest someone with a vivid imagination get the wrong idea.)

As I sat there multitasking it occurred to me that to the countless thousands who passed by in that relatively brief time, I may have looked like a visitor from the future—watching TV on my laptop, talking to my wife face-to-face from a continent away. Yet, of course, I went totally unnoticed by those passing by. In today's wired world, this was just standard operating procedure.

Somewhere in those few minutes, I might have caught a glimpse of the future of football-viewing—accessible, portable, downloadable, and densely detailed.

We've already come a long way. When I first got into the league as an assistant PR guy for the San Francisco 49ers, a primary part of my job during the season was to fly early in the week to the home of our next opponent and spend the better part of the week handing out newspaper reprints and video clips to promote stories and coverage leading up to the game. This was standard procedure in the league for every team. As one league official put it, "The media helps us sell our stuff."

Pete Rozelle built the NFL into the preeminent sports league by consolidating and mechanizing the way each club dealt with the media. The TV networks became their "broadcast partners" and the local media outlets were given unprecedented access, and were even wined and dined to make sure that our "product" was being published and broadcast.

Today, the focus and the mechanism have changed. As in all other business endeavors, the Web has changed the landscape of the NFL and the way it does business with its fans and the media. The sheer number of outlets, primarily via the internet, has made it seem unnecessary for the NFL and clubs to push their product for recognition. The league's primary goal now is to regulate its own "intellectual property," better known as the game.

Mike Greenberg, of ESPN Radio's *Mike and Mike in the Morning*, sums up the perspective this way: "When I started back in Chicago twenty years ago, the attitude of both the clubs and the players were different. They were constantly pushing stories and players at you to promote the games. Nowadays it seems the team PR staffs are nothing more than buffers between the media and the coaches and players trying to regulate the amount of contact to protect themselves against bad press."

There's a feeling around the league that this stuff has become superfluous, but it seems clear to me that, if anything, communicating with fans through the media will be more important in the wired world in which we're living.

Capitalizing on the growth of the internet will have huge ramifications, but few in the NFL seem to have a clear view on just how that will happen.

George Bodenheimer, president of ESPN/ABC, questions

the direction and timing. "It's an evolving medium. I mean two years ago, you didn't have as much video on the internet as you do now and you heard very smart people running big companies saying it's not really a video medium. Now you see there is an explosion of video on the internet, the money is going to drive it." But Bodenheimer, like many, is not sure what the time frame will be. "If it turns out there are business models and fortunes to be made and businesses to be built, I think it could likely take ten to fifteen years to manufacture."

One advantage that sports in general, and the NFL specifically, have in the broadcast world is it is still pretty much "appointment" TV. In a world where advertising executives are grappling with larger and larger numbers of viewers using DVR or taping their favorite shows to view them later, people still prefer to watch an NFL game while it is happening. (Though a spirited minority of people have made it a habit to wait a half hour *after* the game starts to begin watching, then zap through the commercials until they catch up to the real-time broadcast around the fourth quarter.)

Considering it is the most popular sport in America, the NFL remains largely opaque. Scouting and technical data on professional athletes—how players respond to each opponent, and in certain specific situations—is much more available in baseball than in football. This difference has been attributed to baseball's being a game that allows for better quantification, and that's certainly true. But it's more than that. There are more secrets in our game—before it, during it, and after it as well.

In particular, coaches have gotten more secretive. I began the 2008 season with the illusion that on the Friday sit-downs, when as a Fox analyst I would chat with coaches preparing for the game, I might be able to glean more than the average commentator, since I had so recently been sitting in the same chair as the men I'd be interviewing. But it didn't turn out that way.

If football coaches are known for anything, it's singleness of purpose. To Sean Payton or Mike Holmgren, I was just another distraction. All the conversations were cordial, and candid as far as was professionally possible. But no one told me anything on Friday that could get him into trouble were I to repeat it on Sunday. I had several games covering the surprising 11–5 Falcons in 2008, but failed to get any real information from my onetime assistant and present brother-in-law, Mike Smith. And, if I was honest with myself, I don't think I'd have been any different, even with a close friend or relative.

Pro football has always been secretive, but not maniacally so. Back in 1946, during the first season played by the Cleveland Browns, Paul Brown invited the beat writers from the Cleveland papers into his office the day after each game. They would sit in the dark with him and watch the coaches' tape along with him, as he would explain every play, what went right and wrong. The writers were there with the understanding that they wouldn't single out players for criticism, and they wouldn't burn Brown. But they got an invaluable education.

I'm not suggesting that Bill Belichick is going to be inviting the *Boston Globe* beat writer to sit in on Monday's film review any time soon. But I am saying that access to game film (which, of course, is by now digital video) is one of the last frontiers in the education of the football fan. As part of the league's film exchange program, these high-end-zone and sideline shots, in which all twenty-two players on the field are visible, are now shot by the league (to avoid the redundancy of the old system, in which each team shot its own game films) and strictly guarded by the league. Each week, only a few plays make it onto the two strategy shows—ESPN's *NFL Matchup* and the NFL Network's *Playbook*. Yet there are a substantial number of fans who are thirsting for more.

Think of it this way: There are nearly two million fans who subscribe to the NFL's out-of-market service NFL Sunday Ticket through DirecTV. These fans live in cities other than the home of their favorite team, and rather than missing a game or going to a sports bar, they spend three hundred dollars a season to see a full slate of NFL games at home.

Isn't it likely that at least a third of these fans would be willing to pay another hundred dollars per season for an hour-long weekly show breaking down their team's previous game on coaches' tape (and, perhaps, previewing their upcoming opponent the same way)? And aren't there at least two to three times as many fans in their home markets who are rabid football fans but don't need Sunday Ticket because they watch their home team religiously, or have season tickets? Put those together and you've got two million people paying another hundred dollars per year for premium coverage—that's $400 million.

You mention such an idea to people at the league office, and they generally express bafflement that any fans would *want* such information. You mention the idea to football people and they instantly clam up. *We don't need all the extra criticism,* they protest. But this doesn't make sense. People will criticize anyway. Wouldn't it be better if they had more information? People have a much better understanding of the game than they did even a generation ago. They've had the benefit of better camera work, more in-depth discussions of strategy, the perspective offered by peeking into NFL playbooks on the Madden video games, and so forth. Bringing them deeper into the game is the next logical step, and it's even more logical because it could be a moneymaker.

Even for fans who don't desire to know why their team keeps failing to pick up the zone blitz, there is a desire for access. And that is the other great frontier in content.

Of course, sometimes the media outlets are provided by the team themselves. Take a look at one of the most respected and hallowed English soccer franchises, the Liverpool Football Club of the English Premier League. Their "e-season ticket" charges fans about sixty-four dollars per year for internet access to a number of features, as well as full highlights and replays of each and every game. Isn't it likely that American fans would pay the same for a similar package? . . . for a fifteen-minute daily show of team news, down to the injured hamstring on the deep snapper? . . . for access to full replays of all their team's games? . . . for the first interview with the head coach when he comes off the practice field? . . . for a glimpse inside the team's war room on draft day? . . . for a shot of the team as it comes out of its locker room and heads down the tunnel before each game?

Such a widespread "season ticket" package for coverage of particular teams is all the more valuable in light of the rules that are already placed on regular media entities. (Local TV affiliates are allowed only two minutes of team highlights for broadcast purposes after a game, and only six minutes of NFL highlights. Websites are allowed only ninety seconds of any material generated by the clubs by way of news conferences and interviews, and have to pull them after twenty-four hours.) These rules are intended to maintain control, in an omnipresent information world, of the NFL's ability to control and monetize its product.

Consider just a few possible innovations: Because the need for game experience is so great, but the injury risk is so high, there will be a continued push toward applying the same technology used by fighter pilots trained in jet simulators for a virtual reality football simulator, which would combine the strategy of

Madden with the point-of-view perspective of the best simulators. This would be a great way to test a backup quarterback's ability to deal with a surprise, but it would also be a killer app for fans who truly wanted to get "inside the game."

One other promising technology that already exists is to present games in 3-D, as was done in a New York theater in a trial run by the league in 2008. The NFL is clearly intrigued with this idea, but the economics of the technology dictate that it won't take off until it becomes widely available for HD broadcast in the home.

Behind the scenes fantasy football has become a driving force, and possibly a precursor to the way the game will be viewed. Fantasy football fanatics look like stock traders sitting in front of multiple computer screens and TVs to keep up with the players. I can promise you I got more statistical data off the internet generated by gamblers and fantasy players than we as a team could possibly generate on our own. Fantasy football—which started out as a quarterback, two running backs, two wide receivers, and a kicker—is now going into special teams and individual defensive players. If anybody ever figures out a way to score offensive linemen's performance, there's no telling how complex it can get.

And the potential here is great. Premium charges for a game full of isolation shots of skill-position players—all of running back Marshawn Lynch's touches in a game, for instance, or every route that Larry Fitzgerald runs—will allow serious fantasy players to gain better insight into how their players are being used. This seems obsessive, of course, but that's the nature of the game and its followers.

In another five or ten years, I could see the NFL allowing fans to listen in to sideline-to-quarterback communication and plays called in the huddle and at the line of scrimmage.

(Of course, to do so, they would have to cut off coaching staffs on the field and in the booths from any ability to see the live TV broadcast.) Think fans wouldn't pay to know what play was being called before it was run? Or to hear the call in the huddle? The NFL's product is necessarily scarce, but the greatest way to make money in the future will be through providing more access to the existing product. Even though coaches will curse the very thought of this kind of intrusiveness, it is inevitable. At every turn changes in league policy and rules are geared toward making the game more profitable.

The two words you constantly hear, from the networks to owners to league officials, are "transparency" and "inclusiveness." As the league has become focused on ways to monetize the game, this powerful push to draw people in will become unstoppable. In every one of these cases the greater revenue comes with greater understanding for fans, a perspective into the game that has previously been unavailable.

But most of those changes are still a few years away. The biggest change on the horizon is one of structure. The relentless push to monetize the game is also going to lead to expanding the regular-season schedule.

To get a sense of where things may be going, it helps to start with the smallest top-secret project you've never heard of. In summer 2008, people at the league were whispering about an internal study called Project Alpha. It was a fancy name for "How do we make fans give a damn about the preseason?"

Coaches insist on the necessity of the games because they're building a team but even for serious fans, there are few things longer than the fourth quarter of a preseason football game. Project Alpha was given the mission of adding meaning to the preseason. Making the preseason more than it is has become a higher priority in the past ten years, as coaches have grown even more cautious about using their starters and, especially, their star players in meaningless games. Early in my head-coaching career I referred to a preseason game as an "exhibition game." I promptly got a call from the league warning me not to use that term again. Alpha was an attempt to find ways to make the games matter to fans when the outcomes clearly did not.

Predictably, one thing Project Alpha made clear was that the best way to make preseason games more desirable is by having fewer of them, and more regular-season games instead. In August 2008, we began seeing trial balloons indicating that the league was looking at moving from a sixteen-game to an eighteen-game regular season. It was a logical corollary to the preliminary conclusions of the Alpha Project, as well as the need to "grow the game" in a stagnant economy. And the math was great: Take away two of the preseason games that are loathed by fans, networks, and players alike, and add two more weeks of the regular season.

This sounds excellent in theory, and you can easily work out the schedule ramifications and sort out the contingencies. It all works except for one thing: Every single football person you talk to is not just opposed but *vehemently* opposed. I spoke to one assistant coach of a team who'd lost half its defensive starters to injury during the first half of the 2008 season, and he just shook his head and said, "I can't even *imagine* adding two games to the regular season."

In 2008 the New Orleans Saints, thought by many to be a Super Bowl contender, had 209 games missed by starters due to injury. Most people don't understand the degree and frequency of injuries suffered by NFL players. It's a crisis right now, even though players are generally in the best shape in the history of the game, and we're playing a sixteen-game regular season. (Proponents will say, "Well, they play twenty games already—we're just moving two more into the regular season." But of course, the starters don't actually *play* in those preseason games to any great degree, so it's adding more full-speed hitting to an already staggering load.) Now you're going to add two more games, another 12.5 percent to the season's duration?

Well, yes. Eventually.

Those who were most enthusiastic about the idea are much lower-key about it than they were not long ago. As one league executive said to me at the Super Bowl, "Yes, we have had some resistance from our football people. We'll obviously be proceeding carefully, and be mindful of their concerns." One half measure I've heard suggested is bumping the schedule to seventeen games first (with the extra game being an interconference game and, for competitive reasons, giving all the AFC teams the extra home game one season, and all the NFC teams the extra home game the next season).

But if we've learned anything about the new group of owners, it's that they're not interested in the timid approach. So you can look for the proposal to add two more games—along with adding, I would think, a minimum of four more roster spots (fifty players dressing out each Sunday, from a fifty-seven-man roster) for each club. That's 128 more jobs for the union, and a significant bump to the TV package, starting in 2011 or 2012.

At the end of the day, I have yet to hear a compelling case that adding one or two games to the regular season will make the game better. It will add revenue, surely, and it forces owners to add roster size, which will please players. But it won't make the game better.

There's a perfect symmetry to the season now: thirty-two teams, sixteen games, eight divisions, four teams in each division. The regular season is a marathon with a purpose, and with only four division champions and two wild-card teams, the regular-season games have an urgency and a weight that no other professional sport can match. An eighteen-game regular season doesn't promise to improve either the quality of the play or the competitiveness of the division races. So, it's coming, but everyone should be clear about it. It's coming for one reason, and one reason only: more money.

Besides adding games, the NFL is looking to add fans around the world. The first steps have already been made, with London Bowls—regular-season NFL games played in London's Wembley Stadium—in both 2007 and 2008. Despite the commercial failure of NFL Europe, the actual appeal of the NFL has grown significantly in Europe, especially in England and Germany. In the future, look for the league to play two or even three games in London, with an eye to adding an expansion franchise there one day.

The Buffalo Bills are already building a base in Toronto, and the Dallas Cowboys (and, to a lesser degree, the Houston Texans) are now very popular in Mexico. One of the driving forces behind the move to put a team in Los Angeles is the league's urge to reach the Hispanic audience of Southern California and beyond.

There are real possibilities for growth in both Canada and Mexico, although the NFL has to be careful in Canada not to be seen as crushing the Canadian Football League, which, especially in the absence of NFL Europe, has served as a minor league for NFL clubs.

In Japan, which has a love for quintessentially American imports like rock 'n' roll and Disney, American football is an even bigger hit. There's even a long-running Japanese anime series, *Eyeshield 21,* about a Japanese student who tries out for, and excels with, a football team in his school. But what is preventing the game from growing further in Japan is that Japanese fans of American football are sophisticated enough to insist on *real games*, not exhibition games. Japan poses an even greater travel challenge than England, but one that isn't insurmountable.

A fully internationalized NFL might play two to four games a season overseas, with the combatants rotating by year, as a way to bolster the audience for the game overseas. The travel is a bear, but it would be handled as it was with the last two London games: Teams would play the game before their bye week, so the jet lag after the game would have less consequence.

Put these pieces together—more access to teams through the internet, more "premium" media streaming on computer, smart phones, and digital cable to prime subscribers, more transparency in preseason games, more regular-season games, a growing presence overseas—and you have the makings of a lucrative, growing National Football League for years to come.

You don't have to look that far into the future to see a new schedule in place, in which international travel for NFL teams is taken for granted, in which player rosters are pushing toward sixty, in which training camp and the preseason become an abbreviated, month-long sprint. And in which the regular season—eighteen games over nineteen weeks rather than sixteen games over seventeen weeks—still starts the Thursday after Labor Day. Adding two weeks would also put the Super Bowl into the third weekend of February, on Presidents' Day weekend, which would drop the unofficial national holiday right in the middle of an official national holiday weekend, give most people the day off after the Super Bowl, and not incidentally, push the highly rated league championship games into the sweeps month of February.

It's a bright future, and it will be thrilling to watch the game continue to grow, bring people together in this country, and win a generation of new fans around the world.

Unless, of course, there's a strike or a lockout in 2011, in which case all long-range planning is out the window, all the momentum that the league has enjoyed for the past twenty years is shot to hell, and all the goodwill that the NFL has generated from its incredibly loyal fan base is potentially squandered by the collective hubris of the people entrusted to take care of the game.

It has always been true, but never more so than now, given today's economic environment: People are not interested in seeing billionaire owners argue with millionaire players over the fans' money. They just want their game.

THE SOUL
OF THE GAME

I may return to the field and coach again one day. If I do, it will be with a heightened appreciation for the game, the people who run it, the men who play it, and the loyal fans who make it all possible.

We're all dealing with a finite number of years. And, in a way, it's even harder for coaches to be told their time is up than it is for players. These relationships that I've built within the game have sustained me for all of my adult life. But even when all the perks that go along with being a football coach go away, the game compels me. I have watched countless hours of football in my life. And it still fascinates me.

I was down in Tampa for Super Bowl XLIII, doing some work on this book and for the NFL Network. But Saturday morning, the day before the game, I took a plane back to Baltimore and my home. I was certainly interested in watching the game, but I didn't really want to sit in the stands, in the same stadium where I'd coached the Ravens in the Super Bowl eight years earlier. It was fascinating to be a part of the Super Bowl extravaganza in the same city where I had been oblivious to the external goings-on the last time around. At Super Bowl XXXV, other than going to practice and a brief fly-by to the Commissioner's Ball, I never left the hotel the entire week.

The day after I got back to Baltimore, Kim and I had some friends over on Super Sunday. For a few hours, we were just fans. We marveled at Larry Fitzgerald's terrific body control and monster second half (127 yards receiving, two touchdowns) for the Cardinals. We gaped at Ben Roethlisberger's elusiveness and ability to create something out of nothing for the Steelers.

And then, at the stirring finish, we sat in amazement.

For days afterward, I'd see people and they'd say, "Wasn't that a great game?"

And I agreed that it was.

Of course, one of these days, next year or the year after that, there will be a Super Bowl that doesn't have such a pulsating finish, one that ends 24–7 or thereabouts, and people will grumble that it was a "dud Super Bowl." I occasionally feel the need to remind people that, while I'm glad they enjoyed it, there *is* no script. The drama in a football game is organic and emerges from two equally matched teams struggling desperately for the upper hand.

The events that most indelibly marked the past two Super Bowls—David Tyree's miracle catch for the Giants in 2008, James Harrison's impossible, clock-beating hundred-yard interception return, and Santonio Holmes's crucial toe-tapping game-winning catch for the Steelers in 2009—were bolts of athletic genius at once unpredictable and unrepeatable.

In fact, the Super Bowl has been on a run of good games for much of the past decade, with six of the last eight games decided by seven points or less.

This is not an accident; it's a direct result of the structure of the league.

Teams in the Super Bowl tend to be very evenly matched.

All of the trends of the last few years—frantic finishes, major upsets with top seeds dropping, thrilling Super Bowls—speak to the work of competitive balance. In other words: The individual games aren't scripted, but the competitive balance that leads to so many closely fought games is a matter of design.

And competitive balance doesn't come about just because the NFL shares more revenue than any other professional sports league, though that helps. Revenue sharing comes about because there's a hard salary cap that teams can finesse and forestall, but cannot break.

As the 2009 season drew near, both sides talked as though the possibility of a year without a salary cap in 2010 might be worth a try. This is a $7 billion game of chicken to the parties involved, but to the fans of the game, it goes beyond that. The 2009 season could be the last year of football as we know it.

If the NFL goes into 2010 without a salary cap, both sides would be taking a terrible risk. Players will lose a lot of the built-in advantages of the present system: free agency that is offered to players after four seasons wouldn't be offered until after six; there would be limits on the number of free agents that the most successful teams could sign; and, perhaps most important, there would be no leaguewide team payroll minimums, so it's possible that total salaries could go down rather than up in the absence of a cap (and certainly the pay disparity between superstars and average players would increase sharply).

It's a risk for the owners as well. Their willingness to remove the linchpin of the modern system—a hard cap—in favor of an unchecked system that would allow a few of the wealthiest owners to spend even more wildly than they already do threatens to tear apart a system that the league is justifiably proud of.

I spoke to one league executive in the spring of 2009, and

asked him what he thought would happen without a cap in 2010. He was both frank and cautious. "I don't think that's knowable at this point," he said. "I honestly think it all depends on what happens in 2010. I know this: There's no owner who wants to shut the business down. They'd really have to be pushed. The union will really have to push them to get there.

"But I stay up night after night wondering, How can we avoid this? How can we keep this game going? We just don't know what's going to happen in 2010."

That's the problem with the positions that both sides seem to be taking: They are staking the future of the negotiations, and thus the game, on little more than an educated guess. No one *knows* what an uncapped year would mean. And so no one knows how it would play out. I just know this: There will be less than a month between the end of the 2010 season and the deadline for a deal. That's not a long time.

So this is a particularly crucial period in the history of the sport. I know the rookie salaries are out of hand. I know that players get a huge chunk of revenues. I know that owners are facing unprecedented debt loads. But if I had to name the biggest single argument in favor of the existing agreement it might be this: Each side thinks it favors the other—and yet it has indisputably served all concerned so well.

Winston Churchill once remarked, "No one pretends that democracy is perfect or all-wise. Indeed, it has been said that democracy is the worst form of government except all those other forms that have been tried from time to time."

I wouldn't be surprised if, a few years down the road, the various constituencies of pro football have a newfound appreciation for the present collective-bargaining agreement. Of course, by then it will be too late. The small problems will long since have become big ones. And the flaws in the system that need fixing will no longer exist, because the whole system will have been blown up. And people will look back longingly at the most recent golden age of the NFL, from the mid-nineties to the lockout of 2011. And everyone, from players to owners to coaches to the infuriated fans, will wonder how it happened. Some will blame the greedy owners. Some will blame the greedy players. Some will lay it at the feet of Commissioner Goodell or the NFLPA's DeMaurice Smith. But the recriminations will be pointless and unsatisfying, and all concerned will still wonder why the people who had worked so tirelessly and with such vision to create and sustain the NFL couldn't keep it together.

It's good to remember, for everyone in football, that this rare position of primacy we have is not a birthright. It's not written into law that we as a country have to drop everything on twenty consecutive Sundays, then spend two weeks building up to the great party weekend, the civic holiday of the Super Bowl.

It's that sense of community evoked by the game that is perhaps pro football's greatest asset. It brings people together across age, race, class, and religion in a way that very few things in modern American life do anymore. That's a good thing. Like the best movies or books or songs, the game works on many levels. People can enjoy it for the intricate details, or for the rooting interest, or for the sheer spectacle, or for all of these things.

I don't want to lose that. I don't want to lose the great passes, the breathtaking catches, the big hits, the sustained drives, the stunning interceptions, the festive pageantry, the preening wide receivers, the spirited gang-tackling, the enforcer linebackers, the commanding quarterbacks, the deafening roars.

Most of all, I don't want to lose that collective feeling that begins on Fridays, for players and fans alike, and percolates through the beginning of the weekend, building to a crescendo as kickoff nears on Sunday. On the field and in the stands, we are unified and we are focused.

The game belongs to all of us. But we have entrusted it to the leaders. All we can do is worry. I sincerely hope that my worry is misplaced. I hope that whatever shape pro football takes in the future, it retains its distinctive communal spirit, its intrinsic fairness, and the sense that any team—smartly assembled, well coached, cohesive, and motivated—has a chance to compete.

If they can retain that, then the commissioner, the owners, the union chief, and the player reps all will have done their jobs by preserving and protecting the future of the game. And pro football will move forward into a bright future, continuing to be what it has been for so many fans: a magnificent spectacle, a civic treasure, an absorbing science, a wonderful art form. In short, it will continue to be more than a game.

ACKNOWLEDGMENTS

This book emerged from our discussions in the winter of 2008 about trying to present a window into what is becoming an increasingly complex and opaque game. As often happens when two people who love football sit down and start talking about it, the conversation expanded from there, and the result was this record of Brian's yearlong exploration of the game, inside and out.

Many were crucial to bringing about this collaboration, but three entities stand out. Michael's agent, Sloan Harris at ICM, understood the project quickly and found the right home for it. Sloan was a valuable guide and sounding board throughout, and was again aided by his marvelous assistant, Kristyn Keene.

At Scribner, we found an enthusiastic and perceptive publisher, with marvelous editing direction by Colin Harrison, as well as oversight from Susan Moldow, associate publisher Roz Lippel, and editor in chief Nan Graham. We're also grateful for Colin's sterling assistant, Jessica Manners; publicity chief Brian Belfiglio; production editor Katie Rizzo; and the design support, including the handsome cover from Rex Bonomelli and the clean, elegant book design of Erich Hobbing.

Then there was Fox Sports. Brian's work as an analyst for Fox gave him the opportunity for this football odyssey, traveling around the country and seeing the game from a variety of different perspectives, talking to the key figures in the NFL about the state of football. It also was a year of learning about the TV business, with invaluable insight from Ed Goren, David Hill, Bob Stenner, Sandy Grossman, Jeff Gowen, Fran Morrison, Dick Stockton, Thom Brennaman, Brian Baldinger, Troy Aikman, Joe Buck, and Bob Broderick.

The crack staff at NFL Films also provided support and guidance, especially Mike Rosenstein, Mark Chmielinski, and Sterling Sharpe. Greg Cosell of the NFL Network was a valuable conduit in addressing the strategy of the game. Eternal thanks to Howard Katz for mentoring Brian through both the book and a new career, and to Andrea Kremer and Fred Gaudelli at NBC, as well as George Bodenheimer at ESPN/ABC.

There are too many coaches, general managers, scouts, agents, and players to thank individually, but we are particularly grateful to Ozzie Newsome (who good-naturedly agreed to separate interviews with both Brian and Michael), Bill Polian, Ernie Accorsi, Steven Ross, Kevin Byrne, Dick Vermeil, Tony Dungy, Bill Cowher, Marty Schottenheimer, Denny Thum, and Mike Smith. Around the league, we received plenty of help from many at the club level, with Bob Moore in Kansas City, Craig Kelley in Indianapolis, and Rick Smith in St. Louis going above and beyond the call of duty.

Several people in the NFL offices were open and accommodating, but we are particularly grateful to Greg Aiello, Mike Pereira, Peter Ruocco, and of course at the top of the list, Brian's longtime friend and partner Ray Anderson.

Thanks also to all the people quoted in the book—as well as all the people who chose to remain anonymous—for their time and insight.

Brian wants to give special thanks to Greg Roman and Vic Fangio, for their in-depth studies on trends in offense and defense, and Megan and Melaine McLaughlin for their help with endless transcription.

Brian also wants to thank his mother—who is much more likely to approve of his language while calling games than she is of his language while coaching games. Finally, no accomplishment would be possible or worthwhile without the loving support of Brian's wife, Kim, and his daughters, Aubree and Keegan.

Michael would like to thank Rob Minter and Kevin Lyttle, both of whom read an earlier version of the manuscript and offered valuable suggestions, as well as Larry Kindbom, Daron Roberts, Brian Hay, Greg Emas, Pat Porter, Bob McGinn, and Rich Moffitt. Special thanks to all who put him up along the way: his mother, Lois MacCambridge, in Chicago; Holly and Joe Tominack in Baltimore; David Zivan in Indianapolis; and Trey, Tyler, and Ashley Gratwick in Kansas City.

Michael is especially thankful to his children, Miles and Ella, who know all about winning games on the road (and who traveled to Green Bay, Indianapolis, Chicago, Kansas City, and Dallas during the writing of this book), and to Ivy Tominack, for her loving support—and gourmet meals—back home.

—BHB/MJM

Baltimore/St. Louis, July 2009

ABOUT THE AUTHORS

BRIAN BILLICK spent nine seasons as head coach of the Baltimore Ravens, where he led the team to a 34–7 victory over the New York Giants in Super Bowl XXXV. Prior to coaching the Ravens, he served as the offensive coordinator of the Minnesota Vikings. In 2008, he joined Fox as a commentator and the NFL Network as a contributor. He lives in Maryland with his wife and family.

MICHAEL MACCAMBRIDGE is the author of the award-winning *America's Game: The Epic Story of How Pro Football Captured a Nation* and *The Franchise: A History of* Sports Illustrated *Magazine*. He has also served as editor of the *New York Times* bestseller *ESPN SportsCentury* and *ESPN College Football Encyclopedia*. The father of two children, Miles and Ella, he lives in St. Louis.